earthsummit.biz

earthsummit.biz

The Corporate Takeover of
Sustainable Development

Kenny Bruno and Joshua Karliner

FOOD FIRST BOOKS

Oakland, California

Text design by Jeff Brandenburg/ImageComp
Cover design by Amy Evans McClure

Library of Congress Cataloging-in-Publication Data on file with publisher.

ISBN 0-935028-89-7

Printed in Canada

10 9 8 7 6 5 4 3 2 1 — 02 03 04 05 06

DEDICATIONS

For Maria
—JK

For Mel, Fran, Beth, Benjy, and Toni
—KBA

Contents

Preface

On Halloween, growing up in New York and San Diego, we used to take bright-orange boxes door-to-door with our friends. "Trick or treat for UNICEF" was the singsong that was our introduction to the United Nations. After the candy collecting and egg-and-shaving-cream fights were over, we sent our pennies to UNICEF. We believed we were partners with the United Nations.

Looking back, we don't know if we really raised much money for the world's children or if it was just a clever marketing scheme, but we certainly believed that the U.N. stood for goodness itself, for peace and helping poor children, and we were proud of this partnership.

These days, "partnership" with the U.N. has a different connotation: it is primarily a description of the effort to get business and industry to help the U.N. in its mission. The primary U.N. partnerships are not with candy-collecting kids, but with global corporations.

Now that we are raising our own families in the twenty-first century, one of our struggles is to inoculate our kids from the corporate values prevalent—to put it mildly—in our society. Between school, TV, movies and clothes, it is hard to resist the daily bombardment of commercialism on our children.

When the United Nations embraces corporations that commodify fun, news, sports and virtually everything else imaginable, companies that define our own children as consumers and target them as potential life-long customers, it's a bit hard to reconcile the reality of the U.N. with the inspiringly long line of flags on First Avenue in New York, or the little orange penny boxes for UNICEF.

When we talk about the United Nations to audiences involved with the anti-corporate globalization movement, we get some puzzled reactions. The first reaction is from those who believe that the U.N. is a tool of U.S. imperialism, which cannot and will not deviate very far from U.S. policy. Many in this group will tend to protest the U.N.'s actions, rather than work to save the organization. The second group are those who point out that the U.N. is the same collection of governments doing all the things we dislike in international politics, including abusing their own people and corruptly rewarding their elites.

Both of these groups are correct. As Phyllis Bennis has documented thoroughly in her book, *Calling the Shots,*[1] the U.N. was created to be a tool of U.S. policy; the U.S. has dominated the U.N., to varying degrees, since its founding. The governments that comprise the U.N. are also the governments that run the WTO, that fund the

World Bank and borrow from it, that privatize electricity and water, that ignore their most impoverished citizens, that oppress minorities and that commit genocide.

A third group, with another interpretation of the meaning of the U.N., sees it as more than the sum of its parts. This group reads *United* Nations, not United *Nations*, and thinks less about the failures of the U.N., however undeniable, and more about the hopeful impulse behind one of the more amazing documents in history, the Universal Declaration of Human Rights.

For this group, the U.N. is about the values of peace, security, human rights, dignity, ecology and health, believing the U.N. could and should become a counterforce to the WTO, currently the most powerful intergovernmental organization in the world. When the world's governments come to their senses, it will be the U.N. that provides the forum for placing human values above the corporate values of the WTO.

Intergovernmental organizations are complex, layered creations, just like national governments. The U.N. will never be perfect, but its Charter starts with the words "We the peoples"—and it is we the peoples who should govern ourselves and therefore the U.N. The U.N., for all its faults, remains the only option at the intergovernmental level for reestablishing the rights and values of people as paramount to the rights and values of corporations.

Our effort to get to the heart of these questions and issues, this book chronicles the growing entanglement between the United Nations and corporations, from the first U.N. Earth Summit in Rio de Janeiro in 1992, to the second Earth Summit in Johannesburg in 2002.

Both of us attended the Rio Earth Summit as part of our work with Greenpeace International. It was in Rio that we witnessed the powerful influence of polluting corporations on the U.N. effort to save the planet. Ever since then we have been working as part of our organization, CorpWatch, with allies from around the world, many of whom are part of the anti-corporate globalization movement, to address this cozy relationship between the U.N. and business.

We hope that this book helps people better understand the direction the U.N. has taken. We also hope that this work will support the United Nations in fulfilling its potential to hold corporations accountable on a global scale.

—New York and San Francisco, June 2002

PART ONE

Perilous Partnerships

CHAPTER ONE

The Globalization Decade

The world's governments, facing a deteriorating planet, are under pressure to save the Earth. The industrialized countries of the North and the developing countries of the South, meeting under the auspices of the U.N., scramble to reach a global deal that will combine environmental protection and poverty alleviation. But a group of global corporations are claiming that *they* have the answers to the planet's environment and development woes. President George Bush sides with the corporate approach. Is the year 1992 or 2002? Take your pick.

The 1992 Earth Summit in Rio de Janeiro represented a high point of hope for the future of the world's environment, and the billions of people who live on this small planet. Gathered amidst Rio's contrasting splendor and misery, more than one hundred heads of state agreed on a series of accords in what was then billed as "the last chance to save the Earth."

The first Earth Summit was aimed at protecting the planet's environment and improving life for the most impoverished of its human inhabitants. The Summit's negotiators produced agreements on climate and biodiversity, which established binding frameworks for tackling some of the world's most serious ecological threats. In addition, the several-hundred-page text known as Agenda 21 set forth a series of guidelines that have served as tools for local environmental movements to use to pressure their governments into taking action on key issues, from halting forest loss, to preserving the rights of indigenous people, to managing and preventing toxic waste.

World leaders, U.N. diplomats, nongovernmental organizations and, to some extent, the general public, emerged from the first Earth Summit in Brazil with a deepened understanding of the connections between the twin crises of environment and development. The output: an action plan outlining how to solve the problems. Yet ten years later, little progress had been made, necessitating a second Earth Summit. The World Summit on Sustainable Development (WSSD) in Johannesburg, South Africa, was to be both a review of the first Earth Summit and an attempt to build on the letter and spirit of Rio. Unfortunately, the governments negotiating Earth Summit II had a steep hill to climb; they were confronted by the stinging reality that in the ten years since Rio, the global ecological balance had deteriorated and world poverty had deepened. In that time, the so-called "sustainable development" solution languished on the margins of an international politics dominated by anti-environmental forces.

And while a man named George Bush occupied the White House once again, the political climate into which WSSD was born was entirely different than that of the first Earth Summit a decade before. Framed by war and terrorism, a significant global recession, a spate of corporate bankruptcies and the U.S. government pulling out of international treaties left and right, the Johannesburg Summit found itself in a very different context than Rio. In the decade between the two Earth Summits, corporate globalization had also consolidated itself through the establishment of the World Trade Organization. Because of this changed political climate, much of the WSSD negotiating text took a step backward from Agenda 21, diminishing the substance of the original Earth Summit agreements. By the time organizers reached the fourth and final preparatory meeting in Bali, Indonesia, many activists began to wonder if the world would be better off without the Johannesburg meeting at all. Midway through the second week, the Indonesian People's Forum decided to boycott the Bali preparatory meeting, and international NGOs grumbled about walking out of the entire process as well. Consumers International, Friends of the Earth, Greenpeace, World Wide Fund for Nature and others said the process was "sinking in a sea of indecision and intransigence," and that "hardly any country can leave Bali without embarrassment."[1] Even the Chair of the meeting, Emil Salim, said the failure to reach an agreement in Bali showed "a lack of good faith and the spirit of constructive dialogue."[2]

In addition to this difficult political climate, Earth Summit II was haunted by the ghost of the first Earth Summit. Much of the spirit of Rio had been killed in Rio itself, when the negotiations mangled the idea of sustainable development almost beyond recognition. The idea of linking "environment" and "development" had its conceptual benefits, but, in the end, the Summit's failure to properly define the terms and the overwhelming corporate influence on the words' meaning corrupted the original concept. Sustainable development was originally defined as meeting the needs of the present generation without compromising the ability of future generations to meet their needs. However, in Rio, "needs" were not defined, leaving overconsumption by the richest corporations and individuals untouched.

Moreover, despite the protest of many nongovernmental organizations (NGOs) present at the Rio negotiations, the Earth Summit documents declared that free and open markets are necessary prerequisites for achieving sustainable development—in these documents, sustainable development was essentially equated with wealth creation. With this philosophy at the forefront, saving the environment and ending poverty were made compatible—on paper—with corporate globalization. In reality, globalization has only exacerbated the world's ecological travails. When confronted with the obvious contradictions between global markets and sustainability, negotiators blinked in Rio, and then blinked again in Johannesburg.

The first Earth Summit also failed to confront corporate power in any meaningful way—this despite the fact that it was becoming increasingly clear that confronting corporate power and changing corporate behavior must be at the top of the international agenda. By 1992 evidence had emerged that found global corporations at the root of most global environment and development problems. A U.N. Centre on Transnational Corporations report documented that transnational corporations generated more than half of the greenhouse gasses emitted by the industrial sectors with the greatest impact on global warming.[3] Transnational companies also controlled 80 percent of the land worldwide cultivated for export crops and dominated production of almost all major toxic chemicals. At the time, just twenty companies controlled 90 percent of pesticide sales.[4] Global fishery corporations roamed the seas, their high-tech, large-scale factory fleets making a hefty contribution to a growing crisis in which 70 percent of the world's conventional fish stocks were either fully exploited, severely overtaxed, declining or recovering.[5] And while a number of factors contributed to the rapid deforestation of both tropical and temperate zones, timber transnationals played a major role as commercial timber harvests increased by 50 percent between 1965 and 1990.[6]

These companies have always argued that they merely are serving government and consumer needs. It is true that governments and consumers are complicit in the irresponsible consumption of fossil fuels and other environmentally damaging goods. Yet global corporations are not mere observers. They are both producers and consumers of these products. They choose which technologies and products to develop. They use their political power to prevent technological transformation and to protect their industries economically, while influencing and even buying scientific and public opinion through marketing and public relations. Notwithstanding the role of the individual consumer and small businesses, global corporations are at the very heart of the unsustainable practices that shape our economies.

Yet governments in Rio allowed big business to avoid mechanisms to control corporate activities, opting instead for a voluntary approach to sustainable development. As we shall see in Chapter Two, some of the world's worst corporate polluters were given special access to the Earth Summit process, establishing a trend of U.N.-corporate collaboration that has only grown since that time. In Rio, Greenpeace International, Third World Network and a number of allied organizations warned that business's heavy influence on the Summit would lead to the "partial privatization of the United Nations," and the "globalization of greenwash."[7] Unfortunately, that prediction may have been right.

As Chapter Three will document, the decade between the two Earth Summits, the United Nations has increased its dedication not to reining in socially, environmentally and economically destructive and unaccountable corporate power on the world stage, but rather to building partnerships with global corporations and advocating corporate responsibility or self-regulation as a solution.

Nevertheless, the U.N. is still the only global institution that is a potential counterbalance to the World Trade Organization and the corporate-globalization regime. Its vision reflects the aspirations of many, placing fundamental values like human rights, labor rights and the environment before corporate profits. In practice, elements of the U.N. still help hold corporations accountable. As Chapter Four argues, this is especially true in the case of a series of international environmental treaties, two of which, the Climate and Biodiversity Conventions, emerged from the Rio Earth Summit.

Corporate Globalization Since Rio

The decade between the two Earth Summits has been disastrous for the twin causes of environmentally sustainable and socially just development. When seen in the context of world events in the 1990s and the beginning of this century, the Earth Summit process is, despite the hype, a mere historical footnote to the dominant trend of corporate globalization. Prior to the first Earth Summit, there was much hopeful and idealistic talk about building a post–Cold War world that fostered ecological sustainability, human development and democratic governance. Unfortunately, the end of the Cold War did not usher in the dawn of the green era for which many in Rio wished and worked; rather, it marked the onset of a globalization process in which transnational corporations worked closely with the world's most powerful nations to put in place an international system of governance that values commercialism, corporate rights and "free" trade above environment, human rights, worker rights, human health and justice.

The post-Rio decade will go down in history as a time in which this new form of global governance, based on the interests of global capitalism, was institutionalized. This new architecture is embodied by the North American Free Trade Agreement (NAFTA), which came into force in 1994, and by the advent of the World Trade Organization (WTO), established in 1995 out of the Uruguay Round Negotiations of the General Agreement on Tariffs and Trade (GATT). Whereas the Rio agreements were meant to protect nature, the WTO and NAFTA rules give transnational corporations favored access to natural resources, while weakening the ability of governments to protect these resources or to legislate in favor of recycling, marine mammal protection and clean air.

Both the NAFTA and GATT negotiations were well under way during the Earth Summit negotiations in 1991 and 1992. Those negotiations cast a shadow in Rio, as U.S. and European governments, responding to a major lobbying effort by the International Chamber of Commerce, took care to ensure that Agenda 21 and other documents were made consistent with these free trade accords' new rules and that the Earth Summit documents were rendered toothless. The Earth Summit and its vision of sustainable and equitable development were not to become a countervailing force to the new, extremely powerful, fully enforceable free trade regimes.

Since then, the WTO has used its enforcement powers of economic sanctions and its antidemocratic secret dispute resolution process to subordinate environment, labor rights and human rights to the newfound "rights" of corporations to trade and invest freely around the world.[8] As a result, the WTO has marginalized the much weaker environmental agreements forged in Rio and dissipated the energy the Earth Summit inspired. The overwhelming momentum of corporate globalization and the power of the free-trade regimes have also made it extremely difficult for participants at Earth Summit II to revive the sense of hope and optimism present ten years earlier.

To a significant degree, the macropolitical story of the 1990s is summed up by the phrase "Marrakech trumped Rio."[9] (Marrakech was the site of the meeting that concluded the Uruguay Round of GATT and established the WTO.) In other words, the U.N. was sidelined as the WTO became the most powerful intergovernmental institution in the world. The rise of the one-dollar-one-vote institution over the one-country-one-vote body mirrored and reinforced a rise in the power of the U.S. in the post–Cold War era, a time when U.S. contempt for the U.N. was still at an all-time high.[10]

Meanwhile, over the last decade, transnational corporations have used the new global architecture to fortify their economic muscle and political power, while lobbying for and receiving much of their desired natural resources, work forces, market access, investment opportunities and global trade rules. Riding the globalization wave—a swell they themselves helped generate—these corporations have increased enormously in terms of size, numbers and sheer power. At the time of the Rio Earth Summit, there were 37,000 transnational corporations in the world, with over 200,000 foreign affiliates. Merely eight years later, their ranks had swollen by more than 40 percent, to 63,000. The number of foreign affiliates quadrupled, to 800,000.[11]

When one compares their revenues to the gross domestic product of different countries, many of these corporations are larger than nation-states. For instance, Royal Dutch Shell's revenues are greater than Venezuela's gross domestic product (GDP). Using this measurement, Wal-Mart is bigger than Indonesia and General Motors is roughly the same size as Ireland, New Zealand and Hungary combined. Overall, 51 of the world's 100 largest economies are corporations.[12]

Over the last decade, using systems of political patronage to garner significant influence in their home countries' governments, these corporations, which now account for about two-thirds of all world trade, have helped shape global economic rules and institutions, to their economic advantage. This has been at the expense of local economies, cultures and industries and often to the detriment of the environment, workers and human rights at the local, national and global levels.

Who Runs the WTO?

Supposedly, each of the WTO's 134 member countries has an equal say in governance. In practice, decision-making is dominated by the "Quad": the U.S., the European Union, Japan and Canada,[13] where three-quarters of all transnational corporations are based.[14] Each member of the Quad represents its corporations' interests at the

WTO. These corporations are often directly involved in writing and shaping WTO rules. In the U.S., this is achieved through official "Trade Advisory Committees," which the private sector dominates. For example, the U.S. International Trade Administration's Energy Advisory Committee is made up exclusively of representatives of giant oil, mining, gas and utility corporations, including ChevronTexaco, Halliburton, Freeport-McMoran and, until recently, Enron.

Using Trade Advisory Committees and corporate organizations, such as the Business Roundtable, the International Chamber of Commerce and the Transatlantic Business Dialogue, corporations have helped create rules that former WTO Director General Renato Ruggiero has called "the constitution of a single global economy."[15] Unfortunately this "constitution" undermines much of what came out of Rio, belying the assertion in the Earth Summit texts and in various corporate manifestos that free trade and sustainable development go hand in hand.

Since it was created in 1995, the WTO has ruled every environmental policy it has reviewed an illegal trade barrier that must be eliminated or changed. With one exception, the WTO also has ruled against every health or food safety law reviewed. There might have been even more anti-environmental rulings were it not for the tendency of nations to water down their policies to meet WTO requirements, even before challenges.[16]

NAFTA has generated booming industrial development, but little investment in the environment. As a result, environmental pollution and related public health problems have increased on both sides of the U.S.-Mexico border.[17] Natural resource extraction is also accelerating in Mexico as a result of NAFTA. In the first four years of NAFTA, fifteen wood-product companies, including International Paper and Boise Cascade, set up shop in Mexico, cutting down some of North America's largest intact forests.[18]

WTO rules, with help from International Monetary Fund (IMF) and World Bank structural adjustment policies, have pried open developing country economies, facilitating a rapid escalation in corporate investment. Foreign direct investment in developing countries increased nearly five-fold in the first eight years after the Earth Summit, jumping from $51 billion to $240 billion.[19] With some of the largest investments coming from oil, coal and auto corporations[20]—and with these investors often receiving subsidies from institutions like the World Bank[21]—environmental and social problems are actually increasing with this globalization of capital.[22]

Once again, Mexico is an important example. Seventy-five percent of Mexico's population lives in poverty today, compared with 49 percent in 1981, before the country underwent reforms that paved the way for NAFTA.[23] The number of Mexicans living in severe poverty (less than two dollars a day) has grown by 4 million since NAFTA began in 1994—despite the significant increases in corporate investment in Mexico.[24] Overall, the absolute number of people living in poverty rose in the 1990s in Eastern Europe, South Asia, Latin America and the Caribbean and sub-Saharan Africa—all areas that came under the sway of free trade policies and/or IMF structural adjustment programs.[25]

Meanwhile, although the industrialized governments in Rio pledged to reduce Third World debt—a problem that keeps countries mired in poverty and that exacerbates environmental problems—the total debt burden in developing and former socialist countries has climbed by 34 percent since the first Earth Summit, reaching $2.5 trillion in 2000.[26]

Similarly, industrialized nations pledged to increase bilateral aid in order to promote sustainable development. Yet, aid spending has declined substantially since the first Earth Summit, falling from $69 billion in 1992 to $53 billion in 2000,[27] and although a decade later these same governments, attending a U.N. gathering in Monterrey, Mexico, once again pledged to increase aid, skepticism is in order, as history shows that such promises have a habit of evaporating once the world's attention wanders.

The Color of Money: Environmental Politics Since Rio

The fundamental need to radically change production and consumption patterns and practices in the North—a concept central to the Rio Earth Summit negotiations—has been all but ignored for the past decade. For instance, instead of reducing consumption in the United States, whose 4 percent of the global population gobbles up a whopping 25 percent of the planet's resources, auto corporations built more sport utility vehicles (SUVs), which pump ever-greater amounts of global warming gasses into the atmosphere.

At the same time, many of these corporations hypocritically touted themselves as "green citizens" in their public relations and advertising campaigns. Environmental good news became fashionable, and these companies were attempting to bring us the good news message so ardently wished for by the entire planet. Unfortunately, believing the good news simply was not warranted. There are some steps forward, but at the global level, they are far outnumbered by steps backward.

Being the bearer of bad news is an occupational hazard for environmentalists, and it is a role that is easy for the public to tire of.

Nevertheless, it is a fact that in the decade between Earth Summits I and II, environmental destruction in much of the world accelerated. Forests dwindled, fisheries declined, and deserts encroached on ever more agricultural land. Potentially hazardous genetic pollution from biotech agriculture contaminated food crops, and clean, fresh water became increasingly scarce. With the 1990s becoming the warmest decade on record, the threat of global climate change loomed ever larger on the horizon, pointing toward a future of sea-level rises and the devastation of entire coastal populations, increasingly severe and frequent storms, environmental refugees, droughts, floods and disease.

The United Nations Environment Programme (UNEP) confirms that the "state of the planet is getting worse."[28] The agency also pins at least some of the responsibility on business, saying "there is a growing gap between the efforts of business and industry to reduce their impact on the environment and the worsening state of the planet."[29]

Both consumers and corporations are complicit in the consumption orgy that is dooming our planet. Raising individual awareness and reducing consumption at the household level is popularly identified as a major solution to environmental problems. Yet there is a limit to the power of the individual. The average citizen can bring a reusable shopping bag to the grocery store, but cannot rent a solar-powered apartment, nor buy a hydrogen-powered car. The individual consumer's power to steer investments toward low-impact products and clean technologies is dwarfed by that of the collective power of major corporations. Whether the motivation is simply to serve consumer demand or whether that demand is created by marketing, the fact remains that transnational corporations are already leading perpetrators, as manufacturers and marketers, of most of the world's environmental problems, ranging from climate change, to overfishing, to forest destruction, to toxic pollution, to pesticide poisoning.[30] Corporate globalization has only increased environmental destruction. As globalization opens investment opportunities for the forest, fisheries, chemical, nuclear, mining and agricultural industries in developing nations, transnational corporations that have depleted the resources or created toxic disasters in their home countries or that can produce goods more cheaply in the developing nations move in, often decimating local resources and impoverishing those people and cultures who have lived off them in a sustainable fashion for generations.[31]

This dynamic also contributes to the growing global trends of climate change, biodiversity loss and toxic pollution. According to Martin Khor, Director of the Malaysia-based Third World Network, the dominance of the globalization paradigm in the post-Rio era has created a situation where "transnational corporations have generally and rapidly expanded the outreach and volume of their activities. This has correspondingly increased the damage caused to the environment in terms of volume and geographical spread."[32]

Despite some gains over the past decade, the growth and globalization of the problems far outstripped the progress. There are some bodies of water and a few cities' air that are cleaner now than ten years ago. Some highly toxic chemicals have been banned or phased down. The use of wind power has increased. The Worldwatch Institute points to a number of social and environmental advances since Rio, including "declining deaths from pneumonia, diarrhea and tuberculosis."[33] International treaties such as the Biosafety Protocol, the Kyoto Protocol and the accord on persistent organic pollutants (POPs) have evolved during this time. However, the single-most important environmental achievement Worldwatch can point to is "the phasing out of production of ozone-depleting chlorofluorocarbons (CFCs) in industrial countries."[34] Yet the phase-out of CFCs was agreed to via the Montreal Protocol—an agreement locked in well before the Rio Earth Summit. Meanwhile, according to Worldwatch, "global emissions of the greenhouse gas carbon dioxide climbed more than 9 percent" since Rio, and "27 percent of the world's coral reefs are now severely damaged, up from 10 percent at the time of the Rio Earth Summit."[35]

The Rio Summit was supposed to promote the transfer of environmentally sound technology from North to South (from highly industrialized to "developing" nations); but globalization's new trade and investment laws, including WTO patent regimes, has kept the acquisition of such technology either too expensive or inaccessible for many Southern governments and companies. A clear example of where technology transfer has fallen down—or been steamrollered by the forces of corporate globalization—can be found in what is supposedly the greatest environmental success in the past decade: the Montreal Protocol to Protect the Ozone Layer. As Martin Khor writes:

> Third World firms find it difficult to have access to substitutes for chlorofluorocarbons (CFCs), chemicals used in industrial processes as a coolant, that damage the atmosphere's ozone layer. This hinders the South's ability to meet commitments under the Montreal Protocol. . . . Under the Protocol . . . a fund was set up to help developing countries meet the costs of implementing their phaseout, and the Protocol includes articles on technology transfer to the South on fair and favorable terms. Indian

firms that manufacture products (such as refrigerators) with CFCs found it very difficult to phase out the use of these substances because of the lack of access to environmentally acceptable substitutes controlled by Northern multinationals. . . . They face closure if they are unable to meet the dateline of eliminating CFCs use by the year 2010. However, the pledged technology transfer on fair and most favorable terms has not materialized. . . . The patent rights to the substitute [for CFCs] are held by a few multinational companies. Some of the Indian companies are willing to pay the market price or even higher for the technology. But a multinational holding the patent has refused to license it unless it can take a majority stake in the companies' equity.[36]

The corporate globalization process has not only broken the promise of environmentally sound technology transfer, but also guaranteed the exact opposite, partially because the Rio Summit failed to define "environmentally sound." This failure allowed established companies to define their own technologies as "sound" and developing countries to call for any transfer at all, under the logic that if a technology came from the North it was more advanced and therefore more environmentally sound. The WTO and its trade and investment laws, the lending policies of institutions like the World Bank and tightening environmental controls in the North have all encouraged the increasing North-South migration and expansion of hazardous industries, such as nuclear, chlorine, coal and tobacco. These factors indicate a trend of de facto North-South transfer of environmentally destructive technologies that were previously the scourge of the wealthiest nations.[37]

The failure of significant technology transfer to occur, let alone the transfer of environmentally sound technology, is related to the decline in promised aid for sustainable development. These broken promises, says Martin Khor, have "inevitably been seen as a lack of commitment and sincerity of Northern governments to implement the Rio agreements and has robbed the UNCED [United Nations Conference on Environment and Development—as Rio was formally known] follow-up processes and institutions of their status and legitimacy."[38]

The ten years between the two Earth Summits have also shown that, despite their eco-rhetoric, for most corporations in the world green is nothing more than the color of money. Greenwash—the phenomenon of socially and environmentally destructive corporations attempting to preserve and expand their markets by posing as friends

of the environment and leaders in the struggle to eradicate poverty—
has become standard operating procedure for most corporations riding on the globalization bandwagon.[39]

Greenwash is everywhere. It's most visible when comparing the
reality of a corporation's environmental record with the rhetoric and
eco-images in its advertising campaign (see Part Two), but it's also
significant in the realm of international politics. Many corporations
that are architects of ecologically and socially destructive globalization
accords (like the WTO) claim to be advocates of sustainable development. They claimed this first in Earth Summit I and again ten years
later, at Earth Summit II. But as a coalition of environment and
development groups wrote about the largest global business lobby, the
International Chamber of Commerce:

> There is a disturbing gap between their self-proclaimed
> commitment and the reality of a consistent record of lob-
> bying to block, postpone or weaken progress in interna-
> tional negotiations on issues of crucial importance to
> sustainable development. Examples include the Basel
> Convention on trade in toxic waste, the Kyoto Protocol
> and the Convention on Biodiversity.[40]

Shell Games

Tracking the behavior of Royal Dutch Shell from Rio to
Johannesburg is particularly instructive in drawing out how global
corporations have pursued a pro-environment and human rights pub-
lic-relations strategy on the one hand while continuing to be deeply
engaged in severely destructive activity on the other. At the first Earth
Summit, Shell's Senior Managing Director joined the World Business
Council for Sustainable Development (WBCSD)—a consortium of
corporate chieftains who sought to portray themselves as part of the
solution to the world's environmental ills, rather than the center of the
problem. As part of this effort, the WBCSD published a book,
*Changing Course: A Global Business Perspective on Development and the
Environment*, which we will discuss in further depth in Chapter Two.
Part of the book was dedicated to "best practices" case studies in sustainable development. Shell's contribution was about "human resource
development" in Nigeria and included this paragraph:

> Foreign direct investment from a multinational corpora-
> tion is often the most effective way of exchanging the
> skills and technologies needed to further sustainable

development in developing countries. In particular, foreign investors can contribute directly to the building of local management expertise and employee expertise through training programs. This has benefits not only for the company concerned, but also for the wider community.[41]

While some may have gained skills working in the Niger Delta's oil fields as a result of Shell's "sustainable development" strategy, it is clear that the then-second-largest oil corporation in the world's definition of sustainable development included extracting well over $30 billion in oil from operations in the Niger Delta region since 1956.[42] Conveniently ignored in this best practices case study, of course, is the fact that Shell has also created a social and ecological disaster in the Niger Delta that has become a classic case study of the horrendous impacts of oil on people and the environment. Very little, if any of the $30 billion went back into the communities of the Niger Delta, where schools and health clinics are hard to come by, and where toxic contamination from oil spills and gas flares fill the water and air.[43]

The heinous conditions in the Niger Delta did not keep Shell from brazenly trumpeting its commitment to sustainable development in the region. The Shell best practices case study explained in *Changing Course* that, as a result of its training program, "quality and safety standards would not be compromised, and good environmental management would be enhanced."[44] But as Ken Saro-Wiwa, a novelist and leader of the Ogoni people in the Niger Delta wrote, the reality on the ground was quite different than Shell's Earth Summit greenwash:

> Shell has waged an ecological war in Ogoni since 1958. An ecological war is highly lethal, the more so as it is unconventional. It is omnicidal in its effect. Human life, flora, fauna, the air, fall at its feet, and finally, the land itself dies. . . . Generally it is supported by all the traditional instruments ancillary to warfare—propaganda, money and deceit. Victory is assessed by profits, and in this sense, Shell's victory in Ogoni has been total.[45]

Three and one-half years after the Rio Earth Summit, Ken Saro-Wiwa and eight other Ogoni were executed by the Nigerian government. Subsequently, evidence emerged that Shell, the target of Saro-Wiwa's criticism, was complicit in his death.[46] After Saro-Wiwa's hanging, the Nigerian military dictatorship cracked down on dissent in Ogoniland. As Naemeka Achebe, General Manager for Shell Nigeria said, "For a commercial company trying to make investments, you need a stable environment. . . . Dictatorships can give you that."[47] In that one crude phrase, Achebe revealed the harsh reality behind Shell's slick sustainable development rhetoric.

In response to the massive public criticism around its role in Nigeria, Shell moved beyond greenwash in an attempt to whitewash its human rights image. Conveniently forgetting the years of complicity with apartheid,[48] Shell began pointing to its support for political prisoners. Seeking to recast itself as a protector of civil liberties, it posted the Universal Declaration of Human Rights on its website, which had the gall to point to Nigeria as a positive example of its human rights advocacy. Using the technique of blatantly co-opting the message of one's critics, Shell featured a photo of a pro-Ogoni rally on its website.

Human rights violations and local ecological destruction were not the only things flowing out of Nigeria along with Shell's oil. The release of methane from massive gas flaring, a practice prohibited in Shell's home countries of England and The Netherlands, as well as in most industrialized countries, combined with the burning of the oil exported from Nigeria, were helping make Shell a significant contributor to climate change.[49] As public concern around global warming grew, it presented another environmental public relations problem for Shell in the 1990s.

Efforts such as the Climate Convention, signed at the Rio Earth Summit, and the Kyoto Protocol, which evolved from it, threatened the future economic viability of Royal Dutch Shell Corporation and the rest of the oil industry. As a result, these companies have become intensely involved in the Kyoto Protocol negotiations, working to water down the global effort to address climate change, the greatest environmental threat in the twenty-first century. For instance, Shell sent forty-three official representatives and lobbyists to the November 2000 climate negotiations at The Hague, a delegation larger than those sported by most countries and nearly half the size of the 100-plus person U.S. delegation. All the while, Shell claimed that it was offering constructive proposals to help save the world's climate (see Chapter Six).

Those with experience dealing with Shell on the local level believed otherwise. S. "Bobby" Peek, a winner of the prestigious Goldman Environmental Prize and representative of the South African organization groundWork, told a press conference at The Hague that

> until we exposed them, Shell lied about their refinery emissions in South Africa for forty years. Today Shell's

toxic pollution continues to poison local communities in a democratic South Africa, and contribute to the company's global carbon emissions. If they lied to their neighbors about emissions in South Africa, how can we begin to believe their rhetoric at the climate change negotiations?[50]

In fact, on closer examination, Shell's activities at The Hague were more focused on developing ways to profit from the Kyoto accord's pollution trading and "clean development" mechanisms, than on creating measures to stave off global warming. As it worked to shape the Kyoto accord inside the halls of the U.N. negotiations, Shell took out a full-page advertisement in the *Financial Times* declaring, "action needs to be taken now, both by companies and their customers," and pledging to reduce its own greenhouse gas emissions.[51] As the Greenwash Snapshot in Part Two of this book shows, this was a fine step, but not nearly as significant as it might have seemed. Like the other fossil-fuel giants, Shell's impact on the climate stems not from its use of oil and gas, but from its production of the commodities: oil produced by Shell accounts for more of the global-warming gas carbon dioxide than most countries in the world, including Canada, Brazil and Mexico.[52] Through public relations and advertising, Shell and the rest of the oil industry continue to pay lip service to global warming (or in some cases, such as ExxonMobil's, still deny its validity as a problem). At the same time, they have never slowed their worldwide efforts to locate and produce more oil and gas. If we are to avoid catastrophic climate change, the world cannot afford to burn these fossil fuels.

Shell did not let up in its public relations offensive at Earth Summit II, either. Instead, at the WSSD Preparatory Meetings in New York, Shell continued to tout itself as the purveyor of beneficial projects in Nigeria, passing out glossy booklets even as the Ogoni continued to denounce the company's role. Shell also became deeply involved in industry efforts to influence the negotiations and project a green image. Its former CEO, Mark Moody Stuart, helped found and became Director of the corporate front group created especially for the event—Business Action for Sustainable Development (BASD)—a joint initiative of the WBCSD and the International Chamber of Commerce. BASD, in its own words, was "formed to ensure business rallies its collective forces for the U.N. World Summit on Sustainable Development to be held in Johannesburg." As Moody Stuart put it, "our message going into the Earth Summit in 2002 is that business is part of the solution."[53]

Moody Stuart's message was sophisticated. He urged companies to
support the Kyoto Protocol, support regulations and support renewable energy development. His discourse was, in fact, a lot more environmentally friendly than that of many governments. But then, so was
Shell's discourse on Nigeria prior to the Ogoni scandals. So activists
were skeptical. Shell, they pointed out, had great rhetoric in Rio, also,
but the reality was something else. "It is especially ironic that a Shell
executive is taking this role, because through its actions, Shell became
a symbol of environmental destruction and complicity in human
rights violations in the 1990s," said Victoria Corpuz, Executive
Director of Tebtebba Foundation, an indigenous people's organization
based in the Philippines. "The choice of Moody Stuart sends the message that Business Action for Sustainable Development will be more
about style than substance."[54]

Cooperation or Cooptation?

In Rio, Maurice Strong, the Earth Summit Secretary General, invited
business to advise him on its view, and business eagerly accepted the
invitation. The Business Council for Sustainable Development, which
later became the World Business Council for Sustainable
Development (WBCSD), was formed for this purpose and has been
enormously influential at the United Nations ever since.

As we shall see in Chapter Three, since the late 1990s, under the
leadership of Secretary General Kofi Annan, the U.N.'s embrace of
world business has tightened even further. The new philosophy, building on the Rio Summit's approach, declared, "Confrontation has been
replaced by cooperation."[55] Mr. Annan said, "In a world of common
challenges, the U.N. and business are finding common ground."[56] The
Secretary General encouraged all U.N. agencies to form partnerships
with the private sector. These are some of the same U.N. agencies that
NGOs and citizen movements respect for their dedication to U.N.
values, and include those dealing with the environment, labor standards, refugees, sustainable human development, children, public
health, industrialization, science, education and culture.

Kofi Annan personally has spearheaded the most high profile of
these partnerships, the Global Compact. On July 26, 2000, eighteen
months after he floated the concept in Davos, Switzerland, Mr.
Annan appeared with representatives of some fifty corporations and a
handful of nongovernmental supporters to officially launch the
Compact in New York. Those corporations subscribing to the Global
Compact agreed to voluntarily adhere to nine core labor, environment
and human rights principles (see Appendix A). However, there was to

be no monitoring of corporate behavior and no enforcement of the Compact. Companies were required only to produce their own "best practices" case studies—carefully chosen examples of how they were addressing one of the nine principles.

Not everyone was impressed by the Global Compact. As an alliance of environment, development and human rights groups wrote to Mr. Annan in July 2000, the Global Compact and its cousin partnerships at other U.N. agencies "threaten the mission and integrity of the United Nations" (see Appendix C). The alliance, which included groups like Third World Network, CorpWatch, Women's Environment and Development Organization, Focus on the Global South, Friends of the Earth and International Baby Food Action Network argued that by associating with corporations with poor human rights and environmental records, while failing to monitor these companies' activities, the U.N. was permitting companies such as Nike, Shell, Novartis and Rio Tinto "to gain all the benefits of association with the U.N. without any responsibilities," essentially allowing these corporations "to 'bluewash' their image by wrapping themselves in the flag of the United Nations."

At the core of the controversy around the Global Compact is a conflict between two approaches to the conundrum of overwhelming corporate power in a world desperately needing radical change toward sustainability. The first approach, favored in the Earth Summit processes and the Global Compact, is "corporate responsibility," which refers to any attempt to get corporations to behave responsibly on a voluntary basis, out of either ethical or bottom-line considerations. The second approach is "corporate accountability," which refers to requiring corporations to behave according to societal norms or face consequences. As we shall discuss further in Chapter Four, voluntary corporate responsibility and corporate accountability may be mutually supportive in some circumstances, but in others it becomes clear that the purpose of voluntary corporate responsibility is not to improve the behavior of corporations on behalf of sustainability, but rather to avoid accountability mechanisms that would be more difficult for corporations to control. Earth Summits I and II represent critical moments in the conflict between accountability and voluntary responsibility. In both cases, corporate advocacy for voluntarism won out. In the lead-up to the Johannesburg Summit, corporations pointed to the Global Compact and other voluntary measures as the reason why accountability measures were not necessary.

When one considers the evidence in this book—that many of the U.N.'s corporate partners, who tout their social and environmental responsibility, continue to expand and develop core businesses that are at the root of the environmental problems the Earth Summit processes set out to curb—it becomes obvious that something beyond voluntary measures is necessary. Likewise, when one considers that in the ten years since Rio, transnational corporations have also successfully resisted most environmental challenges, maintaining unsustainable practices in the energy, chemicals, agriculture, extractive, technology and transportation sectors, it becomes imperative that strong accountability measures be developed. Finally, when one considers the Enron debacle and all its consequences, it becomes patently obvious that something is terribly wrong with the self-regulatory route.

One of the central lessons of the Enron scandal is that when left to their own devices, at least some corporations will gravitate toward irresponsible behavior. Enron took advantage of the deregulatory dynamic of globalization to push for a variety of domestic and international arrangements that suited its own bottom line in the short term. As a result, the company ultimately collapsed, affecting millions of employees, investors and consumers around the world. When seen in the light of the Enron experience, the cutting edge of corporate environmentalism at the first Earth Summit—voluntary adherence to principles and self-regulation—now sounds much more like mealy-mouthed rhetoric. The Enron experience makes it clear that the idea of corporations self-policing is patently absurd—be they Enron, ChevronTexaco, Nike, Rio Tinto or Novartis. In light of the Enron debacle, a major effort to request that hundreds of companies support nine principles seems a distraction. The U.N. must be a leading advocate for fundamental reform of the global economy by building mechanisms for corporate accountability.

The Seattle Movement

The Johannesburg Earth Summit coincided with trends such as ongoing corporate globalization, environmental deterioration, deepening poverty and growing U.N. engagement with the private sector. A key question, then, is becoming obvious: Can the United Nations address the root causes of the world's growing environmental problems, thereby necessarily confronting the practices of global corporations, while simultaneously seeking to increase U.N. cooperation with these very companies? In many respects, the worldwide movement challenging corporate-driven globalization has answered this question with a resounding "no!" Gathering steam throughout the 1990s, this broad-based international social movement emerged most forcefully in Seattle, in 1999, when 50,000 people took to the streets to mostly non-violent demonstrations at the WTO ministerial meeting. The Seattle movement was followed by mass protests in Prague, Washington, D.C., Quebec, Chiang Mai, Davos, Porto Alegre and Genoa.

The message rang clear: "Free trade" and globalization, as embodied by the WTO, NAFTA, World Bank and IMF policies and corporate investment practices, undermine democracy, local economies, ecological sustainability, human rights and labor rights. The voice and message of this movement, which has increasingly been echoed by more mainstream critics of the global economy, finds itself diametrically opposed to the corporate-inspired Earth Summit mantra that open markets are a prerequisite for sustainable development. Instead, it has begun to develop an alternative vision—one that is inspired by the slogan "another world is possible."[57]

Part of this vision is for the U.N. to alter its approach toward transnational corporations. Instead of promoting a voluntary, corporate-responsibility model, this new movement advocates that the U.N. become home to a binding legal framework on corporate behavior. Such a framework would hold corporations accountable across the globe. In this way, the U.N. could begin to fulfill its potential to serve as a counterbalance to corporate globalization. It could more effectively promote environmental, labor and human rights. It could help build true global security.

If the U.N. is to achieve this, then large political realities must be overcome, including the reluctance of the U.N.'s most powerful member states. The challenge, already great, will become impossible unless the entanglement between the U.N. and global corporations is reversed.

CHAPTER TWO

The Corporate Capture of the Rio Earth Summit

Just before the first Earth Summit in 1992, Maurice Strong, the event's Secretary General, strode up to a podium in an auditorium at the Copacabana Palace Hotel in Rio de Janeiro. Standing before an audience of corporate executives, environmental managers and the press, Strong rebuked his critics, taking aim at those in the international environmental movement who had chastised him for aligning the Earth Summit—that is, the United Nations' Conference on Environment and Development (UNCED)—with corporations at the root of much of the world's environmental devastation. "The environment is not going to be saved by environmentalists," he baldly asserted. "Environmentalists do not hold the levers of economic power."[1]

In a turn of a phrase, Strong encapsulated a doctrine that has since dominated much of global environmental politics and the United Nations' overall relations with transnational corporations. These relations have spanned not only the gamut of environmental and developmental issues, but also human rights and labor, as well as economic, social and cultural affairs.

The doctrine is this: Instead of monitoring and holding accountable increasingly powerful transnational corporations, the United Nations will seek to partner with these companies, talking them into using their hold on the levers of power to voluntarily comply with universal human rights, labor rights and environmental principles.

Behind this philosophy are two conundrums facing the U.N. The first is how to steer corporations toward environmentally and socially sound behavior when those same corporations are so powerful they can overcome most political attempts to control them. The second is how to confront corporations without losing the all-important support of the United States for the U.N.

These riddles have no easy solution, and one must feel some sympathy for U.N. leaders trying to solve them. But as Indian environmentalist Vandana Shiva has said, "Leadership . . . in the generation of environmentally unsound technologies does not automatically translate into a leadership to generate environmentally sound technologies."[2] The self-evident fact that global businesses must become part of the solution does not mean that they *are* part of the solution today, nor that they will become part of the solution of their own accord and within current market structures. Furthermore, in order to avoid environmental catastrophe, most or all major corporations in certain industries must change most or all of their behavior. It takes blinders to avoid this simple truth while looking at only a few best practices partnerships.

The experiment with voluntary measures and partnerships, an understandable attempt to solve the conundrums facing the U.N., has failed. The rest of this chapter outlines the evolution of this experiment to the present day.

Lessons from the Baby Formula Wars

In the 1970s, giant multinationals became the target of one of the first, and still one of the most successful, international campaigns to change corporate behavior ever undertaken. The best-known company was Nestlé, the Swiss-based transnational food company that was the inventor and is still the largest manufacturer of infant baby formula. In the second half of the twentieth century, Nestlé and others in the infant food industry used a series of aggressive marketing techniques to increase their sales of infant formula and foods including using images of healthy-looking babies in ads, playing on women's anxiety over not producing enough milk, stressing the superiority of their product, getting medical endorsements and giving free samples.[3] By the end of the century, WHO and UNICEF estimated that 1.5 million babies died annually because of failure to breastfeed instead of bottlefeed.[4]

In the 1970s, a group of activists, led in the U.S. by the organization Infact, launched a boycott of Nestlé. As a result, in 1981, WHO and UNICEF adopted the International Code of Marketing of Breastmilk Substitutes, which set international standards for national legislation to hold accountable the infant formula industry. The International Baby Food Action Network undertook an international campaign to get governments to adopt and implement the Code. In reaction to the Code, Nestlé pioneered the art of avoiding international regulations on its behavior—a practice that has become increasingly refined over the years.

As UNICEF consultant Judith Richter documents in her book, *Holding Corporations Accountable*, Nestlé used every trick possible to avoid changing its behavior. It deployed the public relations firm Hill and Knowlton to attack its critics. It derided the Code as anti-free enterprise. It allied with the U.S. to weaken the Code. (The U.S. first lobbied to water it down, and then walked away from it anyway, a pattern that was to become all too familiar; since then the U.S. has used similar tactics with the Basel Convention, the Climate Convention and other international agreements.) Nestlé distorted the meaning of the Code with its own detailed interpretation. It avoided public hearings. Nevertheless, the WHO Code survived this onslaught and succeeded in ridding much of the world of Nestlé and its industry competitors' worst and most abusive excesses. Paradoxically, despite this regulatory success, Nestlé still violates the Code today, while publicly claiming to support it, and infant formula continues to cost millions of infants their lives.[5]

Our purpose here is to note that Nestlé had entered into the U.N.–sponsored negotiations over the Code that would regulate Nestlé itself. While the Code was successful in setting some international standards that helped govern this industry in the name of the people adversely affected by it, Nestlé's behavior still set the stage for corporate strategies in the years to come. The company managed to delay the adoption of the International Code, weaken it and later circumvent it. In the process, Nestlé's techniques included lobbying, partnerships, dialogue, conventional public relations, misinformation and attacks on the integrity of its adversaries.[6] The same techniques were used repeatedly over the next twenty years, as companies attempted to avoid limits to their power and reach.

Death of a Code

Despite the fact that the loopholes Nestlé helped open in the WHO/UNICEF Code were big enough to allow the corporation to literally drive trucks full of infant formula right through them, the international effort to hold Nestlé and others accountable still put the fear of God into the corporate world. The fact was that an international grassroots campaign was able to team up with the U.N. to set standards that imposed a series of norms on a group of some of the largest, most powerful corporations in the world. Corporate concerns, of course, were communicated to and represented by the governments where most of the world's corporations are based—Europe, North America and Japan. Perhaps their greatest preoccupation was not the WHO code, but the fact that part of the U.N. was developing a much broader and more far-reaching Code of Conduct.

The U.N. Centre on Transnational Corporations (UNCTC) was created in the 1970s at the behest of Third World governments who expressed the need for systematized information on foreign corporations investing in their countries. Over the years, the UNCTC produced a series of reports and recommendations on labor, environmental and other issues, such as corporate investment in apartheid in South Africa. By the time of the Rio Conference, governments had spent some fifteen years discussing a Code of Conduct for transnational corporations under the auspices of the UNCTC and the intergovernmental body that created it, the U.N. Commission on Transnational Corporations. (In the years since, the phrase "Code of Conduct" has most frequently referred to unilateral, voluntary and self-generated corporate codes, rather than outside codes negotiated by governments.) The impetus for the Code came mostly from the developing world, with negotiations widely supported by Southern countries and by NGOs. The draft Code had never been very "radical"—in fact, it became increasingly watered down over the years—but the UNCTC's efforts were still seen by many corporations and Northern governments as a potential threat to the ideology of corporate self-regulation they espoused. Pressure increased on the UNCTC (and the U.N. in general) in the 1980s, the Reagan/Thatcher years, when the ideological and political tide turned against more regulation of transnational corporations. The new approach, termed the "Washington Consensus," favored neoliberal or free-market economic policies. However, it was in the early 1990s, coinciding with the lead-up to Rio, that the UNCTC and nearly two decades of these U.N. efforts to set global standards for corporate behavior met their death.

For the Earth Summit negotiations, the UNCTC was asked by the U.N. Economic and Social Council (ECOSOC) to prepare a set of recommendations on transnational corporations and other large industrial enterprises that governments might use when drafting Earth Summit I's central document—Agenda 21. The recommendations had five sections: a) global corporate environmental management; b) risk and hazard minimization; c) environmentally sounder consumption patterns; d) full-cost environmental accounting; and e) environmental conventions, standards and guidelines.[7] But when it came time to present these recommendations in March 1992 at the UNCED preparatory meeting in New York, the UNCTC found itself marginalized.

Just before that, then U.N. Secretary General Boutros Boutros-Ghali announced, as part of his program to restructure and streamline the U.N., that the UNCTC would be eliminated as an independent entity. This move, while purportedly aimed at reducing waste, in effect responded to political pressure to make the U.N. more business-friendly. It also gutted the agency of what little power it might have had. In February 1992, the UNCTC was placed under the Department of Social and Economic Development and reconstituted as the Transnationals and Management Division. (A year later, it was kicked over to the United Nations Conference on Trade and Development, making it more marginal still.)[8] Yet the UNCTC still had the recommendations commissioned by the U.N.'s Economic and Social Council (ECOSOC) to deliver to Maurice Strong and his UNCED Secretariat. Try as the UNCTC staff might, however, they couldn't get the Secretariat to accept their report, which might have laid the groundwork for a set of international standards on corporations and sustainable development.

One of the reasons this happened was that powerful countries representing their corporations' interests opposed the UNCTC's recommendations. As Peter Hansen, former director of the UNCTC, explained:

> The Recommendations were focused on Environment and Development. . . . The U.S. and Japan both opposed them, as they had opposed the Centre on Transnationals. The U.S. and Japan had also made it quite clear that they were not going to tolerate any rules or norms on the behavior of the TNCs (transnational corporations), and that any attempts to win such rules would have real political costs in other areas of the negotiations.[9]

Not only did the UNCTC's Earth Summit recommendations die a nearly anonymous death, but also, by 1993, both the draft U.N. Code of Conduct and the U.N. Centre on Transnational Corporations were gone.

Meanwhile, Strong had appointed Swiss billionaire Stephan Schmidheiny as his Senior Industry Advisor. Schmidheiny proceeded to form the Business Council for Sustainable Development (BCSD, now known as the World Business Council on Sustainable Development—WBCSD) and prepare the book *Changing Course: A Global Business Perspective on Development and the Environment.*[10] The book paints a picture of a rosy future in which corporate environmentalism, based on open markets, free trade and self-regulation, will give birth to global green capitalism. In a sense, *Changing Course* replaced the UNCTC's recommendations; this in turn reflected not so much a major new direction industry was embarking on toward sustainable development (which is how the WBCSD and Strong spun it), but rather, much more importantly, a fundamental shift in how the U.N. interacted with corporations.

Changing Course?

That telling event in Rio, when UNCED Secretary General Maurice Strong dismissed those who argued that the world's most environmentally destructive corporations did not necessarily have the solution to the world's ecological ills, was, in retrospect, an engagement party of sorts between the U.N. and these very companies. It was organized by the WBCSD, a conglomeration of some fifty CEOs from leading corporations such as Royal Dutch Shell, Dow Chemical and Mitsubishi. Through the WBCSD, these corporations initiated a partnership with the United Nations that has grown over the last decade, figuring even more prominently at Earth Summit II in Johannesburg.

As Strong stepped down from the podium, he was followed by the high-tech presentation of a series of "best practice" case studies. Despite the sophisticated visuals, these were crude examples of how a dozen different corporations were taking small steps to reduce pollution, preserve land, help the poor, waste less paper in the office and plant trees. The case studies—which included the example of Royal Dutch Shell's Nigeria operations discussed in Chapter One—were part of *Changing Course*, which WBCSD executives released at the event and which laid out the framework for corporate engagement in the sustainable development debate.

Changing Course articulates a vision of "sustainable development" that, endorsed as it was by the CEOs of corporations such as Royal Dutch Shell, Volkswagen, Mitsubishi, Chevron, Dow and Dupont, has since been adopted by much of the corporate world. This corporate environmentalism is based on four fundamental pillars. First, it contends that unleashing market forces to promote ongoing economic growth through open and competitive trade is the fundamental prerequisite of sustainable development. Second, it calls for pricing mechanisms to correct distortions in the world economy and reflect environmental costs. Third, it argues that self-regulation is the best, most preferable and most efficient method for transforming business practices. Finally, it calls for more changes in technology and managerial practices in order to promote cleaner production and the more efficient use of resources.[11]

These concepts were not entirely new. In the years prior to the Rio Summit, global corporate environmentalism became refined through a series of strategy meetings, fora and conferences, such as the International Chamber of Commerce's (ICC) Second World Industry Conference on Environmental Management in Rotterdam, where a "Business Charter for Sustainable Development" was promulgated in 1991. More than 1,000 corporations signed the nonbinding Charter, which urged that environmental management in a free market setting be recognized "as among the highest corporate priorities."[12]

This ideology of free market corporate environmentalism was taken to a new level with the creation of the WBCSD. The first Earth Summit marked the coming of age of global corporate environmentalism, the melding of ecological and economic globalization into a coherent ideology that paved the way for transnational corporations to reconcile, in theory and rhetoric, their ubiquitous hunger for profits and growth with the stark realities of poverty and environmental destruction.

As it turns out, it was an imaginary world the corporate environmentalists envisioned, one in which the corporate drive for profits, the ecological balance of the planet and people's basic needs would be brought into harmony through market mechanisms. Instead, a decade later, *Changing Course*'s legacy is the "best practice" case study. Corporations have repeatedly used these unverified, carefully selected examples as greenwash tools. The best practice case study allows corporations to portray themselves as part of the solution to the environmental crisis, while artfully skirting central issues such as the overall impacts of their businesses in a country, in an industrial sector or globally. So successful has the introduction of the best practice case study been that the United Nations has made best practice case studies the centerpiece of its Global Compact with corporations (see Chapter Three).

While *Changing Course* was a corporate tome—business's submission to the Earth Summit—Maurice Strong had clearly positioned the U.N. to walk hand in hand down the aisle with these global corporations as they said their vows to become green global citizens. Strong's doctrine, in contrast to the Code of Conduct approach, aimed to foster greater corporate responsibility to the environment and human rights by appealing to the private sector's self-interest. He made the WBCSD's billionaire founder, Stephan Schmidheiny, his special business adviser. Together, they argued that the road to greater profits would be increasingly paved with good intentions. "Either we resist and we will suffer," Schmidheiny said at the time, "or we anticipate the changes and we will have more profits and more personal satisfaction." In other words, unless global corporations moved quickly to "promote self-regulation," Schmidheiny told the business press, "we face government regulations under pressure from the public."[13]

Strong rounded out his doctrine by greasing the wheels of this corporate environmentalist model: He created an Eco-Fund to help finance the Earth Summit. The Eco-Fund franchised rights to the Earth Summit logo to the likes of ARCO, 3M and Mitsubishi Group member Asahi Glass.[14]

Corporate "Diplomacy"

The first Earth Summit's failure to grapple with the impacts of the most environmentally destructive entities on the planet is an important story to tell and an important history to understand if current trends are to be reversed.[15] It is a chronicle of both the demise of corporate accountability initiatives, such as the UNCTC Code, inside the U.N. and the consolidation of corporate environmentalism as a global ideology and practice. It's also a tale of the omnipresent corporate lobby's agile and successful endeavor—led by the ICC—to virtually silence all discussion among governments about the need for international regulation and control of global corporations. And it is a story of how this corporate diplomacy undermined the ability of those negotiating the first Earth Summit to achieve the goals they had set out for themselves of fostering ecologically sustainable development. As Martin Khor, Director of the Third World Network asserts:

> The most glaring weakness at Rio was the failure to include the regulation of business, financial institutions and TNCs (transnational corporations) in Agenda 21 and other decisions. These institutions are responsible for generating much of the pollution and resource extraction in the world, as well as greatly contributing to the generation of unsustainable consumption patterns and a consumer culture. UNCED and the Commission on Sustainable Development, the U.N. system as a whole and governments have collectively failed to create international mechanisms to monitor and regulate these companies.[16]

This breakdown was no accident. According to former UNCTC Environment Unit Director Harris Gleckman, the European Community, Japan and the U.S. launched a frontal assault "to avoid any reference to transnational corporations" in Agenda 21. And in a stunning example of government-corporate collusion, the Canadian government hosted a series of meetings to coordinate the corporate lobbying of the Earth Summit negotiations.[17]

The WBCSD and ICC, who despite some friction for the most part closely coordinated policies, proceeded to demonstrate what self-regulation meant: making Agenda 21's chapter on business and industry compatible with their positions; lobbying, most often successfully, for the elimination of references to transnational corporations wherever possible throughout Agenda 21; and ensuring that the idea of even a minimal system of international regulations never gained public acceptance.

Negotiators took pains to ensure the Earth Summit agreements would be consistent with the trend toward open markets, which was in full swing via the GATT/WTO and NAFTA negotiations. For example, Chapter Two of Agenda 21 states, "The international economy should provide a supportive international climate for achieving environmental and development goals by a) promoting sustainable development through trade liberalization; [and] b) making trade and environment mutually supportive. . . ." This was consistent with the ideology of the ICC, which, one year earlier, in its Charter for Sustainable Development, stated that "economic growth provides the conditions in which protection of the environment can best be achieved . . . profitable businesses are required as the driving force for sustainable economic development and . . . the resolution of environmental challenges."[18]

In general, instead of mandating far-reaching change, the Earth Summit documents ordain that the global fox must guard the planetary henhouse. The World Bank, an institution that continues to receive widespread criticism for its environmentally destructive pro-corporate globalization policies, was effectively put in charge of managing all of the funds generated by UNCED and its conventions.[19] The Bank's energy-lending record since then has been anything but an example of sustainability. For instance, the World Bank has been the primary engine pushing forward a fossil-fuel-based model of corporate globalization resulting in more local pollution and more global greenhouse gas emissions. Overall, according to the Institute for Policy Studies, in the nine years after Rio, the World Bank Group invested $15.7 billion in oil, gas, coal and fossil fuel-power projects around the world, and only $1 billion in renewable energy and energy efficiency. Much of the World Bank's largesse went not to projects aimed at bringing electricity to the poor, but rather to contracts for large fossil-fuel corporations and to serving the energy needs of other corporate investors riding the wave of globalization.[20]

Meanwhile, the Rio documents enshrined free trade, which was to become the flashpoint of the globalization debate, as the sacred icon of sustainable development. The call from the South, as well as from many environmental groups, for a reduction in consumption by the Northern countries was rejected by the North.

The manner in which other aspects of Agenda 21 spoke to the corporate agenda is equally striking. Agenda 21 proposed that forest cover be increased through the expansion of plantation forests, which would provide cheap raw materials for pulp, paper and timber companies, while failing to recognize and support the land and cultural rights of indigenous peoples and traditional forest dwellers. Agenda 21 also failed to address the rampant expansion and industrialization of the world's fisheries. UNCED omitted any discussion of nuclear power, allowing nuclear companies to portray themselves as "part of the solution," even though there are no inherently safe storage and disposal solutions to the world's growing radioactive waste problem. Discussions of the environmental impacts of the military, including the nuclear and toxic contamination caused by military activities around the world, were excluded from the Earth Summit negotiations and texts.[21]

While a number of stray references to transnational corporations did sneak into Agenda 21, the corporations more or less ignored them. For example, former UNCTC official Harris Gleckman observes that during the various meetings of corporate executives held in Rio, there was very little discussion of these references. Instead, these meetings focused on "further expansion of transnational investment and trade on their definition of environmental protection."[22]

Ultimately, the corporate sector was extremely pleased with the results of the Earth Summit. As Jan-Olaf Willums and Ulrich Goluke write in the ICC's 1992 book, *From Ideas to Action:*

> In general, the feeling among business participants was that the substantive output of UNCED was positive. It could have taken a negative stance on market forces and the role of business, and there was at one time the real possibility that the conference might be pushed to lay down detailed guidelines for the operations of transnational corporations. Instead, it acknowledged the important role of business. National governments have now begun to formulate their own policies and programs in accordance with commitments given in Brazil. We expect that these national laws and regulations will not be as stringent, bureaucratic and "anti-business" as some feared before UNCED.[23]

Over the next five years, the entry of business lingo and philosophy into the U.N. system intensified. Whether by inclination or under pressure, the U.N. leadership continued to cultivate business-friendly policies. A moment that was telling in terms of just how much the climate had changed at the United Nations since the days of the UNCTC occurred in June 1997, during the five-year review of the Rio Conference. The mood was dark: The environment was still deteriorating, development had been sidelined on the international agenda and developing countries did not even want to talk about environment until development was back on track. The deal struck at Rio, of "common but differentiated responsibilities" between North and South, had been broken, as financing for technology transfer had not materialized and development assistance was down. Ismail Razali of Malaysia, who was President of the General Assembly, was frank in saying the results were "sobering."[24]

Ambassador Razali had few options for convincing the industrialized countries to take their Rio obligations seriously. Instead, he cohosted a high-level luncheon of lobster and exotic mushrooms with corporate executives from the WBCSD. At the close of the meeting, Ambassador Razali announced that a framework for the involvement of the corporate sector in U.N. decision-making would be worked out under the auspices of the Commission on Sustainable Development.[25]

Despite such high-level success, the big corporations and their industry associations are leaving nothing to chance. The ICC continues to work aggressively to consolidate its gains and fend off any initiatives for corporate accountability. For example, when the Commission on Sustainable Development, which meets annually to monitor and assess the implementation of Agenda 21, came together in April 2001, the ICC sent no fewer than 80 delegates.[26] The Rio Conference also served as a model for other, similar events that were to follow; for example, in 1995, references to transnational corporations were eliminated from the texts of the World Summit for Social Development in Copenhagen, though Preparatory Committee documents had drafted language calling for a Code of Conduct.[27]

The Potential Role of Environmental Treaties

Despite the reluctance to confront corporate influence, the Earth Summit did produce a set of treaties that do require changes in corporate behavior. The international diplomatic realm remains a key battlefield, one through which significant controls have been and continue to be placed on the operations of transnational corporations: For example, the Montreal Protocol to Protect the Ozone Layer, even with its shortcomings, has forced corporations to phase out a series of chemical products highly destructive to life on Earth. Similarly, the proposed accord on Persistent Organic Pollutants (POPs) has the potential to require the phase-out of a slew of highly hazardous chemicals, forcing chemical corporations to be accountable to environmental concerns. The Basel Convention on the Transboundary Movement of Hazardous Waste has justly restricted "free" trade in toxic waste to the benefit of the environment. The Climate Convention looms as a potential wake-up call for the petroleum giants; indeed, the powerful lobbying effort they have launched to stymie this agreement is indicative of the threat it poses to their nearly unrestricted production of fossil fuels. The Biodiversity Convention continues to be a viable vehicle for placing safety restrictions on the global biotechnology corporations, while also guaranteeing a modicum of equity for the stewards of biological resources—mostly Third World farmers and indigenous people who have discovered and catalogued a vast array of plants over many generations.

Thus, while transnational corporations are not directly accountable to the U.N., these agreements, whose viability and effectiveness are always dependent on pressure from below, do provide a forum in which national governments can agree on enforcing internationally coordinated actions to rein in the destructive global reach of stateless corporations. The following is a discussion of the varying degree of success that three agreements, the Basel Convention, the Biodiversity Convention and the Climate Convention (all related in one way or another to Rio) have had in addressing the environmental impacts of global corporations and "free" trade.

The Basel Convention

Before the Rio process started, a troubling phenomenon emerged, calling into question the fundamental belief that trade is good. The phenomenon was a growing international trade in hazardous wastes.[28]

This trade had several notable characteristics relevant to the discussion of sustainable development. First, as both costs and public opposition to hazardous waste disposal grew in industrialized countries, the waste was exported from richer to poorer countries. Second, though waste trade was a commercial trade, it was morally indefensible, because it implied that poor countries had to choose between poverty and poison. Third, though importing waste was a potentially profitable activity, becoming a dump could never be justified as a sustainable development strategy.

In 1989, the first meeting of the Basel Convention on the Transboundary Movement of Hazardous Waste was held. The subsequent Rio documents and Commission on Sustainable Development meetings supported the work of the Basel Convention. In 1994, the Basel Parties, in an historic decision, banned hazardous waste exports from the Organization of Economic Cooperation and Development (OECD), the world's richest countries, to non-OECD countries.[29] The Ban went against the grain by saying, in effect, that trade is not always desirable; some forms of trade are wrong and should be banned.

The Basel Ban does not eliminate all trade in wastes. OECD countries can still trade amongst themselves, and "nonhazardous" wastes can still be traded freely. Recently, old computers from the U.S. have been exported by the thousands of tons to China.[30] Even though the computers contain toxic constituents, they are not defined as hazardous under the Basel definitions. In the fall of 2001, steel from the destroyed World Trade Center in New York was exported to India, apparently without first being tested for possible contamination from asbestos and heavy metals present in the Twin Towers.[31]

Nevertheless, the Basel Convention remains an example of a U.N.-sponsored agreement that does control transnational corporate behavior through its rules on trade. Although such control has not yet become a trend, Basel gives hope that multilateral agreements can reflect environmental and social priorities over commercial trade and investment priorities.

The Biodiversity Convention

The saga of the Biodiversity Convention, which first came to prominence in Rio and which has continued to evolve ever since, illuminates the role that corporations have played—sometimes successfully, sometimes not—in attempting to trump the letter and the spirit of the Rio accords.

Together with the Climate Convention, the Biodiversity accord was supposed to be one of the "jewels in the crown" of the first Earth Summit. However, in Rio, the U.S. biotechnology industry and the U.S. government teamed up at the last minute to oppose the Convention and throw the Earth Summit into some political disarray. While the U.S. originally supported the negotiation of this agreement, aimed at preserving fast-disappearing genetic stocks of plant and animal species, it began watering down the Convention during the years when it was negotiated. Then, in what even the U.S. Delegation Chief and then-EPA Administrator William Reilly called "a perverse twist," the U.S. government discovered that it had such fundamental objections to the agreement that it was compelled to reject it.[32] U.S. President George H. W. Bush justified his 180-degree turn by explaining that "in biodiversity it is important to protect our rights, our business rights."[33]

After the Earth Summit, the U.S. Council on International Business (USCIB) elaborated the theme in Congressional testimony. USCIB representative Jonathan Plaut explained that U.S. business opposed the Biodiversity Convention because it called into question intellectual property laws that allow the biotechnology industry to patent and exclusively profit from genetic organisms often gathered in Third World countries.[34] The Convention's provisions on sharing access to and the "transfer" of this biotechnology back to the Third World, whence the original resource came, ran counter to U.S. corporate and, not coincidentally, U.S. government stances, in what were then the GATT negotiations. According to Plaut, the Biodiversity accord threatened to "undermine the U.S. negotiating position" in the GATT's Uruguay Round, which was not yet complete at the time, but later became the basis for the WTO. Finally, Plaut noted that the American corporations were opposed to language in the treaty that called for regulation of the biotechnology industry.

Bill Reilly, toeing the Bush line, concurred in Congressional testimony, noting that the treaty singled out "the biotechnology industry as inherently risky, unsafe and worthy of special attention and regulation." This threatened "an industry fraught with economic potential, but also environmental opportunity to solve real and important environmental problems. We could not, therefore, agree to that." With this twisted logic of "environmental opportunity," Reilly justified U.S. opposition to the Biodiversity Convention. In a bold move, he actually argued that biotechnology corporations such as Genentech, a subsidiary of the Swiss firm Hoffman–La Roche, have the potential to generate so many environmental benefits that their economic growth shouldn't be stunted by environmental regulation.[35] This, despite the fact that leading scientists argue that the potential hazards to human and environmental health caused by biotechnology merit some kind of precautionary or regulatory control.[36]

The debate over the Biodiversity Convention raged on through the 1990s and into the twenty-first century, as the biotechnology industry continued to grow and develop. With the election of Bill Clinton in late 1992, it appeared that U.S. policy would substantially change. However, once in office, the Clinton administration only created a more sophisticated approach to protecting U.S. corporate interests. The administration agreed to sign the Convention, thus appearing to support the international environmental cause of biodiversity protection, but at the same time, it moved to attach a letter of interpretation to it. The letter, drafts of which were written by U.S. biotechnology corporations, turned on their head some of the Convention's regulatory and intellectual property provisions about which President Bush had expressed so much concern. Given the power and reach of the U.S. government and the biotechnology industry, this statement has the effect of undermining much of the potential effectiveness of the agreement.[37]

The U.S. government continued lobbying for the biotechnology industry during ongoing Biodiversity Convention negotiations, as well as in the U.N. Commission on Sustainable Development (CSD), the official follow-up body to UNCED. It did so by opposing a Biosafety Protocol to the Convention and attempting to suppress discussion in the CSD of any internationally agreed framework for the safe handling and transfer of biotechnology. The U.S. government's influence in the CSD was apparent when, in 1995, a group of scientists and activists issued a statement accusing the CSD of following an approach to the biotechnology issue that was "akin to a public relations exercise for the industry."[38] Meanwhile, despite resistance from the U.S., the European Union and Japan, as well as hard lobbying from the biotechnology industry, delegates to the Convention on Biological Diversity, led by countries such as Colombia, India, China and Malaysia, agreed in late 1995 to establish a protocol on biosafety.[39]

Despite the advent of the Biosafety Protocol, it became increasingly clear that the WTO agreements are the big deterrent to a strong and successful accord. One of the central elements of controversy is the Protocol's advocacy for a global Precautionary Principle to curb the marketing of untested genetically modified organisms. The Precautionary Principle, enshrined in both Agenda 21 and the Biosafety Protocol, stipulates that the lack of absolute scientific certainty should not stop a country from taking protective measures. The Biosafety Protocol was designed to protect human health and the environment in response to the rapid emergence of a new, almost completely unregulated industry: biotechnology. The genetic engineering revolution the world has witnessed since Rio has generated increasing public and scientific concern about the unbridled use of genetically modified organisms in the environment and food supply.

The biotech industry has fought these concerns with a powerful PR campaign (see Part Two) and through international governance structures. The industry has used the WTO, with all its economic might and enforcement powers, to attempt to override the Biosafety Protocol. Meanwhile, by allowing transnational corporations to patent organisms, plants and gene sequences found anywhere in the world, the WTO's patent rights undermine the biodiversity convention's call on signatory nations to "respect, preserve and maintain knowledge, innovations and practices of indigenous and local communities" and the role they play safeguarding these resources.[40]

Many of these WTO rules were practically written by U.S. biotech corporations such as Dupont, Pfizer and Monsanto, along with EuropaBio, a lobbying group representing 600 European corporations. As Canadian analyst Tony Clarke explained, "These new trade rules provide protection for the biotech industry at the expense of policies and programs originally designed to serve the needs of people and the environment in countries both North and South." Indeed, the policies and accords undermined by the WTO's patent rules extend beyond the Biosafety Protocol to food safety laws and public health initiatives—including the pressing need to get affordable pharmaceuticals to AIDS victims in Africa.[41]

Throughout these conflicts, the U.S. government continued to side with the biotech industry. This was clearly illustrated in 1999, when the United States sabotaged the Biosafety Protocol negotiations. Prioritizing the interests of the U.S. biotechnology industry and the multilateral trading system over those of the global environment and human health, the U.S. worked with five allies to almost torpedo an international agreement sought by the rest of the world. "There were two compromises that we were not prepared to make," said U.S. delegate Rafe Pomerance. "One [was] to tie up trade in the world's food supply. The second [was] to allow this regime, without a lot of deliberation, to undermine the WTO trading regime."[42]

Despite the drawbacks and setbacks, and despite the efforts at sabotage by the biotechnology industry and U.S. government, the Biosafety Protocol continues to be an indispensable tool for preventing genetic pollution by controlling corporate behavior in the biotech industry.

The Climate Convention

The other jewel in the crown of the Earth Summit was the Framework Convention on Climate Change, which, several years after Rio, resulted in the creation of the Kyoto Protocol. In contrast to the Biodiversity agreement, President George Bush (the father) signed this accord, which called for the stabilization of the world's greenhouse gas emission at 1990 levels. Nearly nine years later, President George Bush (the son) nearly did this agreement in when, at the behest of the fossil fuel industry, he withdrew the U.S. from the Kyoto Protocol.

The U.S. government's nixing of the Kyoto agreement in 2001 represented a crude payoff to corporate interests. The interim between Presidents George Bush I and George Bush II, which more or less parallels the time period between Earth Summits I and II, has witnessed an ongoing battle, primarily a fight between perhaps the most powerful business sector in the world, the fossil fuel industry, and much of the rest of the planet.

Literally hundreds of corporate lobbyists have descended on every negotiating session since the Kyoto Protocol was established, pushing "market-based solutions" to the climate change problem. These "solutions" have included emissions-trading initiatives that would create a multi-trillion dollar market for the free trade in greenhouse gasses. They have included corporate-friendly (but not necessarily climate-friendly or environment-friendly) schemes with such obtuse names as "Joint Implementation and the Clean Development Mechanism." Ironically, the second Bush administration has pulled out of what the Amsterdam-based think tank Corporate Europe Observatory called "the most corporate-friendly environmental treaty in history."[43]

Among the most-visible lobbying groups at the Kyoto Protocol negotiations were what have become the usual suspects—the ICC and the WBCSD. These two organizations had over 100 and 200 lobbyists respectively accredited to the U.N. climate change conference that took place in The Hague in November 2000, known as COP6. As the Corporate Europe Observatory tells it, the COP6 negotiations were an extension of the corporate politics of the Rio Earth Summit:

> While the ICC put great effort into positioning itself (and business in general) as environmentally responsible, its lobbying efforts aimed to prevent measures which would effectively combat ever-increasing CO2 emissions, measures which the ICC calls "command and control" policies. The Global Climate Coalition, which aggressively opposes the Kyoto Protocol and is widely seen as the most irresponsible business lobby group, used a different rhetoric style, but lobbied on a platform largely identical to that of the ICC, focused on unrestricted emissions trading. . . .

> One of the prime ICC spokespeople in The Hague was Brian Flannery of ExxonMobil, a company infamous for fighting the Kyoto Protocol. With his ICC hat on, Flannery delivered the ICC's rosy "free market environmentalism" discourse to the media. But during COP6, Flannery also spoke out as a lobbyist of Exxon Mobil and

then the feel-good rhetoric was replaced by questioning the scientific evidence for climate change and making warnings against government investments in green technology.[44]

As the corporate lobby continued to pour the pressure on directly at the negotiations and indirectly through influencing the U.S. government and others, global greenhouse gas emissions continued to rise. In addition to the failure of the Kyoto Protocol to come up with strong measures to save the Earth from potentially disastrous global climate change, a reason for the growth of greenhouse gas production was the brand of globalization being promoted by institutions such as the World Bank and the WTO.

The Climate Convention has the potential to affect corporate and consumer behavior profoundly, and for the better. But so far it has not touched the core contradiction of a society dependent on fuel that causes climate change.

In the end, those who purported to be the saviors of the planet at the Rio Earth Summit, the global corporations, have, in fact, continued to reside at the heart of environment and development dilemmas with which the world is confronted. These companies have proved expert at undermining and derailing global agreements with the potential to address substantively these problems by reining in corporate excess. As we shall discuss in the following chapter, the new model of U.N.-corporate collaboration developed through the Earth Summit I process has not only evolved and deepened for Earth Summit II, but also spread beyond the domain of environment and development, infecting the entire U.N. system. Yet despite all the corporate efforts, these international environmental accords have proved stubbornly resilient to the corporate onslaught, and are still one of the world's best hopes for fostering global corporate accountability on environmental issues.

CHAPTER THREE

The Swoosh, the Shell and the Olive Branch

On July 26, 2000, Secretary General Kofi Annan shook hands in front of the U.N. flag with one of the world's most aggressive protagonists of globalization's race to the bottom, Nike CEO Phil Knight. The occasion was the formal launch of the Global Compact, the U.N.'s highest-profile corporate partnership program. With this initiative, the U.N. formally took on board not only corporations like Nike, Novartis, Shell and Rio Tinto, but also the dominant business approach to global social issues.

This approach, first pitched to the global public in Rio by Maurice Strong, was premised on the theory that corporations, including those that are the primary cause of the twin crises of environment and development, also hold the solutions to these crises. Therefore, as the thinking goes, they must be part of negotiating implementation of those solutions. The theory assumed that business expertise in environmentally destructive technologies will translate into expertise in environmentally sound technologies. The message of the Global Compact and other U.N.-corporate partnership programs seems to be that Nike's swoosh and the U.N.'s olive branch logo are compatible, that McDonald's and Disney may represent universal cultural and educational values and that giant oil companies, like Shell, Chevron and BP, hold the keys to sustainability.

In the previous chapter, we saw that the 1992 Rio Summit signified a sea change in terms of the U.N.-corporate relationship. No longer was the U.N. an antagonist to the corporate world; it became a suitor. The U.N. invited global corporations to become openly involved in negotiating solutions to problems of which they were a primary cause. Business, already in the process of developing its own greenwash strategy in order to avoid new regulations on its global operations, eagerly accepted the invitation.

The period from the 1970s to the early 1990s might be considered an era of defensive action by corporations at the U.N. As they worked to minimize the threats the U.N. posed in terms of fostering international corporate accountability, they kept many new regulations off the books, and they increasingly shaped the diplomatic agenda to be consistent with their own aspirations—or at least harmless to their bottom line. They also intervened, with varying degrees of success, in treaties on toxic waste, ozone, climate, persistent pollutants and biodiversity, to water them down or make them more business-friendly. However, in the post-Rio era, from the mid-1990s onward, the corporate world complemented its defensive strategy with some sophisticated offense. A new trend emerged at the core of this offensive—the trend of partnership. As a result, the U.N. and global corporations have become increasingly entangled with one another; business has become an ever more integral part of decision-making at the United Nations. This chapter traces how the early romance between the U.N. and business, which began in Rio, has evolved into the tight embrace of partnership embodied by the Global Compact.

Howdy, Pardner!

Partnership: It's a lovely word. In dance, tennis, love or business, where would we be without partners? In a world where violence and confrontation are fatally destructive, we must welcome the cooperation that partnership implies.

Partnership has come into fashion at the United Nations. While it may be in vogue, it is also terribly vague. Its meaning is so malleable that it can serve almost any master. What is missing from the U.N.'s approach to corporate partnership seems to be an analysis of the motivation of the involved corporations. Such a glaring absence on the U.N.'s part makes these partnerships perilous indeed.

Judith Richter, a former UNICEF consultant who closely studied Nestlé and the infant formula controversy, believes that public-private partnerships are part of an overall corporate strategy of "engineering consent," also known as issues management or just plain corporate public relations.[1] Though clearly not every partnership fits this corporate strategy, it is undeniable that for corporations involved in controversial matters, a partnership with an NGO, such as the World Wildlife Fund, or an intergovernmental agency, like the U.N., can be an excellent cover.

An example of how corporations can hide behind such partnerships came out in 2001, after the airing in the U.S. of an expose called
"Trade Secrets," by U.S. television journalist Bill Moyers. The program gained access to a cache of documents proving beyond doubt
that the chemical industry covered up information about the harms of
vinyl chloride and other chemicals, misleading its own workers, the
government and the public.

After the program, American Chemistry Council Vice President
Terry Yosie dared to come on the air to discuss the show with Moyers.
Amazingly, he expressed not a hint of regret to the victims shown in
the film. Yosie thought Moyers should have pointed out that chemicals are part of modern life and needed for certain products that
Americans buy and enjoy, just one of many disturbing facets of the
industry response to the "Trade Secrets" program. The most relevant
point was the main technique attempted by the ACC—using a phony
partnership to cover up environmental sins.

In his opening statement, the Chemistry Council's Yosie referred
to the industry's "major partnership with one of this nation's leading
environmental groups, Environmental Defense. . . ."[2] Yosie used the
"major partnership" to bolster his suggestion that all chemicals on the
market now are fully tested and safe.

This blatantly misleading suggestion, made on national television,
prompted the Council's supposed partner, Environmental Defense, to
write demanding a retraction. In reply, the Council's President, Fred
Webber, further obscured the topic by admitting Yosie was partly
incorrect on a technical point, but failing to correct his essential mis-
statement.[3]

This exchange should provide a warning to all would-be partners
of corporate polluters. When the going gets tough, these companies
are ready to hide behind the public image of their partners—whether
these partners agree to it or not. Environmental Defense Senior
Attorney David Roe says there was no official partnership with the
ACC. He acknowledges, however, that the two groups collaborated,
along with the U.S. EPA, on the design of a major testing program for
chemicals. Roe points out that the collaboration was sparked by
Environmental Defense's report, "Toxic Ignorance," which showed
that most chemicals had in fact not been tested, at least not to public
knowledge.[4] In other words, the collaboration was entered only when
the industry needed it to fend off criticism.

Not all partnerships are bad—but not all partnerships are good,
either. For a partnership to be successful, there needs to be convergence
of goals, clarity of roles and a balance of power. Yet the corporate part-

nerships which emerged at the U.N. in the late 1990s and early twenty-first century were often missing all or some of these features. The growing coziness between the U.N. and the private sector first became publicly visible in early 1998, when the U.N. and the ICC issued a joint statement after Kofi Annan met with twenty-five corporate leaders and ICC representatives, including those from Coca-Cola, Unilever, McDonalds, Goldman Sachs and Rio Tinto. The statement was based on the belief that the broad global, political and economic changes since the end of the Cold War "have opened up new opportunities for dialogue and cooperation between the United Nations and the private sector."[5] It was also founded with the vision that "there is great potential for the goals of the United Nations—promoting peace and development—and the goals of business—creating wealth and prosperity—to be mutually supportive."[6]

Following this meeting, literally dozens of corporate partnerships sprung forth from the alphabet soup of U.N. agencies, making for some strange bedfellows. UNESCO, promoter of diverse cultural values, jumped into bed with Disney and McDonalds, bastions of cultural homogeneity. UNHCR, protector of refugees, co-convened a forum with Unocal, a corporation whose activities have helped generate refugees.[7] UNEP, steward of the environment, created a partnership with some of the most environmentally destructive mining corporations in the world. And WHO, keeper of the infant formula marketing code discussed in Chapter Two, considered doing a partnership deal with its old nemesis, Nestlé. The partnerships seemed to be emerging pell-mell, with little clear thinking behind some of them and insufficient guidance from the Secretary General's office.

In July 2000, Kofi Annan, together with leaders of some of the world's most powerful corporations and industry associations, launched the Global Compact. The Secretary General's office simultaneously released a set of guidelines for "cooperation between the United Nations and the business community."[8] Together, these two initiatives seemed an attempt to lend some order to the chaos of emerging U.N.-corporate partnerships. While welcome, this systemization also served to institutionalize some of the partnerships' most serious structural flaws.

The Global Compact, which has emerged as the highest-profile corporate partnership at the U.N., has been cited as a model and major initiative by many corporations and U.N. agencies. In the Global Compact, Secretary-General Kofi Annan asked business to abide by nine principles derived from key environmental, labor and human rights agreements (see Appendix A). Virtually everyone involved with the U.N. at any level believes in and promotes these nine principles. But the Compact has serious flaws, not the least of which is the fact that there is no way to monitor, let alone enforce, corporate compliance with the principles they agree to endorse, essentially giving companies notorious for their environmental abuses and human rights violations a free ride on the Secretary General's prestigious coat tails.

As corporations become increasingly ensconced at the U.N., partnership and cooperation are increasingly assumed to be the best approach inside the world body, while "confrontation" is almost a dirty word—this, despite the fact that, as many corporate executives and U.N. partnership boosters privately admit, it is so-called negative campaigning, also known as "confrontation," that drives them toward dialogue, partnerships and even social responsibility in the first place. This partnership approach is one that suits the corporate agenda perfectly, for what better partner could there be for business than the U.N., an international symbol of peace and justice with no monitoring capability?

At the U.N., partnership seems to mean an endorsement not only of specific corporations, but also of corporate economic theory and ideology. As Kofi Annan put it, "The goals of the United Nations and the goals of business can and should be mutually supportive. In today's interdependent world, the United Nations and the private sector need each other."[9] The ideology behind U.N.-corporate partnerships is a belief in the benefits of open markets, which are seen by high-ranking U.N. officials as "the only remotely viable means of pulling billions of people out of the abject poverty in which they find themselves."[10]

The term "open markets" may sound enticing, but, in the real world, it often means that the rules enforced by the WTO are done so at the expense of developing countries, farmers, consumers and the environment. Essentially, this partnership approach fails to address a fundamental divide: the interests of global corporations and the multilateral trading system they have been instrumental in devising on the one hand, and the interests of the world's poor, the environment and democratic institutions on the other. Critics of the U.N.'s new approach have continually argued that the growing concentration of wealth and power in the hands of fundamentally undemocratic global corporations and other institutions of globalization clashes with the U.N.'s overriding purpose: to enhance human dignity and the capacity for self-governance.

There is no doubt that the U.N. must interact with the private sector, and that it must have guidelines for such interactions. The U.N. and its specialized agencies must cooperate with the business community, for procurement and information sharing, for example.

Although ideally governments would provide full funding for all U.N. programs, it is also understandable that U.N. agencies try to mobilize funds from the private sector for certain programs. What is not clear is why "partnership" must be the dominant paradigm for the U.N.-business relationship. Partnership should be entered into by entities that share goals. As former UNICEF head Carol Bellamy has said, "It is dangerous to assume that the goals of the private sector are somehow synonymous with those of the United Nations, because they most emphatically are not."[11] The U.N. has not adequately explained the meaning of partnership with the private sector, nor justified the proliferation of these relationships.

2B2M: The UNDP Steps in It

In 1998, just a few months following the Kofi Annan–ICC call for greater collaboration between the U.N. and corporations, a colleague passed the authors a document that had been leaked from inside the U.N. Development Programme (UNDP). It outlined a new partnership program called the Global Sustainable Development Facility (GSDF), designed, it seemed, by the same players who facilitated the corporate role in Rio. Sitting on the steering committee of the GSDF was Maurice Strong, Secretary General of the first Earth Summit; the group of Senior Advisers to the initiative included Bjorn Stigson, Director of the World Business Council on Sustainable Development and the ICC's Maria Livianos Cattaui.[12]

The GSDF, which was never, as they like to say in U.N.-speak, "operationalized," carried the unfortunate slogan "2B2M: 2 Billion People to Market by 2020." The idea of 2B2M was that the UNDP would "create sustainable economic growth and allow the private sector to prosper through the inclusion of two billion new people in the global market economy." In other words, the UNDP claimed that the lives of the world's two billion poorest people, who have a collective income roughly equal to the world's richest 225 individuals, will be improved by drawing them into a ruthless world economic system dominated by a few hundred giant corporations. The UNDP and its senior advisers apparently saw no contradiction here, asserting, without any substantiation, that "in the long term, a strong relationship exists between sustainable human development and the growth of shareholder value."[13]

This analysis missed a few important details. The most pressing needs of the poor are health, education and food. Poor people, by definition, hold little interest to giant corporations. Providing affordable, clean water, new classrooms and basic foods to poor people are not traditionally profitable businesses. When water and education have become profitable, through privatization, it has tended to restrict access to these fundamental resources, while raising deeply troubling issues for basic rights and democracy. Bringing water and education into the market economy is not likely to win the UNDP many friends among the poor, as the violent struggles over water privatization in Bolivia have shown.[14]

Initial pledges of $50,000 to the GSDF came from Dow, Rio Tinto, ABB and Citibank, companies with policies that harmed not only poor people, but also the environment. According to the UNDP, in return for their support and participation, these companies were to be given access to the agency's network of country offices, high-level governmental contacts and reputation. With the aim of "highlighting the special relationship with UNDP," the U.N. poverty alleviation agency also considered creating a special GSDF logo which would have been used by participating corporations.[15]

Civil society groups were outraged by the GSDF: It gave participating companies a role in the governance of this quasi-U.N. program. The UNDP is also one of the most highly respected U.N. agencies among NGOs, and many of the opponents were themselves UNDP partners. In a meeting with UNDP Chief Administrator Gus Speth, some of these NGO partners pointed out it was the UNDP that had done so much excellent work on microcredit, small and medium enterprises, and so on. This agency, which NGOs admired, was now choosing to partner with the likes of Dow and Rio Tinto. It was also promoting global markets—the same ones that had failed to reach to the least industrialized countries—as the solution for the world's poorest citizens. To many people working for and with UNDP around the world, the GSDF was a slap in the face.

Civil society slapped back. Gus Speth was taken aback when a group of NGOs met with him and expressed dismay at the prospect of the GSDF.[16] When critical articles appeared in the press about the GSDF, UNDP officials took pains to point out that the GSDF was not finalized and had not been launched. However, the UNDP already had guidelines that were supposed to govern its interactions with the private sector. Included was a mandate for a "systematic assessment" of corporate partners. Criteria for such an assessment included:

> [Determining] whether the objectives and practices of a given corporation are compatible with those of UNDP. . . . [Are] activities or products of the corporation compatible with UNDP image and ideals? . . . Are activities or services of the corporation . . . deemed to be ethically, socially

or politically controversial or of such nature that involvement with UNDP cannot be credibly justified to the general public? For example, collaboration with corporations with a reputation of: exploitative involvement in developing nations; illegal financial transactions; drug trafficking; producing or trading in arms; child labor; activities endangering the environment; poor and/or exploitative working conditions for employees; poor gender policies; discriminatory behavior, (etc.).[17]

Given the poor environmental and human rights records of many of its new partners, the UNDP had clearly failed to carry out the thorough research and analysis called for in the guidelines. Neither did the UNDP consider the potential for its new partners to use their relationship to bluewash their image by wrapping themselves in the U.N. flag, something the UNDP guidelines clearly warned about when they stated: "When UNDP is engaged in public relations activity within the framework of a corporate relationship, a mutual image transfer inevitably takes place. If UNDP is prepared to contribute to improving the image of a corporation" it must consider the public image and track record of that company.[18]

The UNDP may have been slightly shaken by the experience of coming under attack by its allies in the nongovernmental world. When Speth stepped down later that year, the GSDF was put in the "deep freezer" and died.[19] The new UNDP Administrator, Mark Malloch-Brown, previously a PR official for the World Bank, formed a civil society advisory committee that included many individuals who were prominent critics of the GSDF. At the same time, the UNDP was becoming more and more business-friendly, partnering with Chevron in Kazakhstan and BP Amoco in Angola, among others.[20] Despite the demise of the GSDF, NGO criticism was not going to derail the corporate partnership train.

One of the worst cases of procorporate bias at the UNDP showed up in their 2001 UNDP Human Development Report (HDR), which endorsed genetically engineered foods and a vision of high-tech, corporate-led agriculture. This was particularly galling to development groups, because previous reports had been seen as among the "few 'official' international documents that challenges [sic] the globalized market-dominated worldview put forward by institutions such as the WTO" and had become important references for pro-poor campaigners.[21] One leading supporter of the UNDP felt that the 2001 HDR was so extreme that it "put an end to the UNDP's image as being pro-poor, pro-environment and pro-human rights."[22] For a

U.N. agency whose mission is to help alleviate poverty and promote "sustainable human development," this was bad news.

What Were They Thinking?

UNDP was not the only agency seeking corporate partnerships in response to Kofi Annan's calls for engagement with global corporations. The rush to partner led to some bedfellows of surpassing strangeness.

Unocal and United Nations High Commission on Refugees (UNHCR)

Former High Commissioner on Refugees Sadako Ogata jointly convened the Business Humanitarian Forum (BHF) with John Imle, then President of Unocal,[23] a company notorious for complicity in human rights violations in Burma.[24] As a partner of the brutal Burmese military government in the Yadana gas pipeline project, Unocal has benefited from forced labor, forced relocation and other crimes carried out for security of the project.[25] Lawsuits against Unocal alleging crimes against humanity are currently underway in U.S. federal and state courts. In one case, the judge found evidence that Unocal knew or should have known that the Burmese military "had committed, was committing and would continue to commit" crimes including forced labor and forced relocation.[26] The dismissal of that case is on appeal in federal appellate court, and a parallel lawsuit in process in California State Court as of this writing.

Although the BHF was not a full U.N. partnership program, the High Commissioner showed remarkable insensitivity by co-convening the Forum and sharing the podium with the head of a company that creates refugees in its business operations.[27] The BHF was founded by a former Vice President of Unocal, yet neither the High Commissioner nor many of the other humanitarian organizations in attendance seemed concerned that it would be used to promote a good image for a company with such a bad reputation.[28] Meanwhile, Kofi Annan gave the whole thing his blessing in the form of a formal greeting to the group's first meeting in early 1999, in which he wrote that he was "particularly pleased to see the business community looking to forge even closer links with our humanitarian work in countries torn by conflict, poverty, famine or natural disaster."[29]

UNESCO and Disney

UNESCO, the United Nations Educational, Scientific and Cultural Organisation, has a number of partnerships with the private sector, mainly in the form of licensing agreements that allow the use of UNESCO's logo or label. UNESCO excludes companies that violate human rights, or make or distribute arms, tobacco or alcohol. Yet it allowed its name to grace the Youth Millennium Dreamer Awards, organized mainly by the Disney Corporation and presented in Disneyland in Orlando, Florida, in May 2000.[30] Obviously, Disney is known for entertaining films and, as is less frequently known, also for its use of sweatshop labor in Haiti, where full-time workers not earning enough to feed their families or send their children to school produce clothing and goods with pictures of Mickey Mouse and other Disney characters.[31]

Disney movies are characterized by race and gender stereotypes, making the company a questionable choice to sponsor Youth Awards.

Mr. Annan Goes to Davos

Many U.N. boosters and employees consider Kofi Annan the best Secretary General ever. His grace is outstanding and his sincerity unquestioned. Kofi Annan is a diplomat, a gentleman and a humanitarian.

Mr. Annan has put his imprimatur, and perhaps staked his reputation, on the Global Compact, which has garnered more attention—positive and negative—than any other corporate partnership program at the U.N. In January 1999, Kofi Annan proposed the Global Compact to a bastion of corporate elitism, the World Economic Forum in Davos, Switzerland. In his speech there, he called on business to "give a human face to globalization,"[32] a twist worthy of the slickest PR operator. Before this speech, the phrase meant exposing the true face of globalization; Charles Kernaghan, the head of the National Labor Committee, an anti-sweatshop group, routinely used the phrase "putting a human face on globalization" to refer to documenting the lives of sweatshop workers in Central America, who sewed jeans and sweaters for the global market. Annan, on the other hand, was urging business to soften the hardest edges of globalization by accepting certain international norms and trying to include the world's disadvantaged. The gap between Annan's and Kernaghan's interpretations of the phrase parallels the chasm of interpretation between proponents and skeptics of the Global Compact.

In Davos, Kofi Annan asked business to embrace nine principles derived from landmark environment, labor and human rights agreements, including the Rio agreements. Virtually all commentators on the Global Compact, including the authors of this book, endorse these nine principles. There is no question they summarize many of the important values the U.N. promotes.

The first step in joining the Global Compact is for the CEO of the company to write a letter to the Secretary General expressing support for the Global Compact. The company must then publicly express that support in its mission statement, annual report, press releases or other similar document. The second commitment is that companies will, once a year, submit examples of progress or lessons learned from putting the principles into practice. An optional activity is to participate in annual Issue Dialogues organized by the Global Compact Office. These are meetings organized by the Global Compact Office around issues such as the business role in zones of conflict or business role in sustainable development. Finally, also on an optional basis, the companies may initiate partnership projects with the U.N. The nature of these partnership projects is not defined, other than that they "help achieve broadly accepted U.N. goals."[33] U.N. officials have gone to great pains to emphasize that the Global Compact is not a membership club, a code of conduct or a regulatory mechanism. It is a network for learning and dialogue.

On the surface, then, the Global Compact is a fairly modest initiative, with only incremental improvements on business-only programs, such as the ICC's 1991 Business Charter for Sustainable Development. Yet it was inaugurated in July 2000 with great fanfare, with the CEOs of corporations such as Nike, Shell, Rio Tinto and Novartis sharing the stage with the Secretary General at U.N. headquarters in New York. Coming as it did in the context of increased corporate influence at the U.N., the Compact raised some bright red flags among supporters of the United Nations. It has also raised some flags in the corporate world, for different reasons. It has garnered some support in the labor movement, and rather more qualified support in the environmental and human rights movements. The Secretary General's Office has been both proud of and defensive about the program.

The differences in perception about the Global Compact come largely from differences in political outlook on the dynamic moment in which the Compact was launched. Throughout the 1990s, with corporate globalization ascendant, citizen movements on all continents rumbled against globalization and its institutions: the WTO, NAFTA, the World Bank and many of the very corporations that helped launch the Global Compact. U.N. officials were more aware than most national governments that a backlash against corporate power and globalization was coming. It did come, in fairly spectacular fashion, at the Seattle meeting of the WTO in late 1999. A crucial clue to the thinking behind the Global Compact is that as John Ruggie, former Assistant Secretary General and an architect of the Global Compact, noted, the Secretary General was prescient in warning business of the backlash against globalization a full ten months before Seattle.[34] Indeed, the U.N. leadership had warned that "opposition to globalization is rising in many parts of the world."[35] In a sense, post-Seattle, Kofi Annan's aides were telling big business: "We told you so."

At the same time, the U.N. said that what was needed was "finding new ways to embed global market forces in universally shared social values, thereby allowing all countries and cultures a sense of ownership in the global economy."[36] There was to be no challenge to global market forces per se, but rather an adjustment better to include social concerns, reflecting a mainstream belief that globalization is essentially beneficial and merely needs some tinkering to improve the distribution of benefits.

For global justice campaigners, the meaning of Seattle and subsequent demonstrations was quite different. Seattle meant a crisis of legitimacy for leading institutions of globalization, including the corporations themselves, as the public came to the realization that corporate-led globalization was the cause of growing inequality. In the wake of Seattle, many, including Kofi Annan, had feared that "there may be a threat to the open global market, and especially to the multilateral trade regime."[37] With the Global Compact, he was offering a tool for re-establishing the legitimacy of major corporations as good global citizens, so as to maintain the trade regime. Or as a *Washington Post* editorial termed it, the Global Compact was a "softener" that could help dull globalization's harsh edge, prevent a backlash and improve the distribution of benefits.[38] By offering corporations the Global Compact as a soft, easy way out of what had suddenly become the globalization conundrum, many in the movement believed that the Secretary General had chosen sides in the globalization debate at a moment when the doors were potentially opening for much more substantial change.

This suspicion was confirmed at the Geneva Forum 2000, when Annan said that the world's poor were suffering not from too much globalization, but from too little. Martin Khor, Director of the Malaysia-based Third World Network and one of the leading thinkers of the antiglobalization movement, countered, "We must oppose the form of globalization that exists."[39] It is significant that Khor is one of the U.N.'s biggest boosters; Khor advocates that the U.N. hold a place at the pinnacle of international governance on trade, environment and development issues.

Smuggling the Business Agenda into the U.N.

In 1991, the authors of the ICC book *From Ideas to Action* expressed surprise that 230 companies had quickly signed on to the Business Charter for Sustainable Development's sixteen principles.[40] Similarly, the Global Compact Office expressed satisfaction that "hundreds" of companies support the Global Compact's nine principles.[41]

A great deal of *From Ideas to Action*, as well as many other publications by the ICC and WBCSD, was dedicated to promoting "best practices." When stripped of fancy phrases like "learning synergies" and "participatory platforms," the Global Compact Learning Forum is clearly dedicated to a similar approach, albeit with the potential of improvement through independent evaluation. Bells and whistles aside, the essential elements of the Global Compact—voluntary commitment to principles and submissions of case studies—recycle a failed business approach to sustainable development. In this case, recycling is not an environmentally sound principle.

Perhaps it is not entirely surprising that the Global Compact is so similar to previous business approaches to voluntary corporate responsibility. The research group Corporate Europe Observatory (CEO) documented that the ICC has been the primary partner and co-designer of the Global Compact. CEO even calls it the "U.N.-ICC Global Compact."[42] In July 1999, the ICC and U.N. issued a joint statement endorsing the Global Compact and saying that "a stronger private sector worldwide . . . is already making an effective contribution to the attainment of United Nations goals." The statement noted that the Global Compact would reinforce "the collaborative partnership between the United Nations and the ICC that is now well established."[43]

For Kofi Annan, this was an important step: the ICC had called for a stronger United Nations. The business endorsement was probably a crucial piece of the campaign to get the U.S. to pay its billions in arrears, one of Mr. Annan's primary goals. A month earlier, the Secretary General had attempted to enlist the U.S. Chamber of Commerce to pressure Congress to pay the money it owed, while promising to "continue to make a strong case for free trade and open global markets," as part of the Global Compact.[44] The Global

Compact became one of Mr. Annan's relatively few cards in a high-stakes political poker game.

From the point of view of civil society, however, the news that the ICC would be the primary partner in the Global Compact was discouraging. As we saw in Chapter Two, the ICC was the leading lobby group aiming to weaken U.N. agreements, such as the Climate Convention and Convention on Biodiversity, both of which came out of Rio.[45] It is significant that this weakening of U.N. agreements by the ICC occurred simultaneously with the evolution of its U.N. partnership.[46]

No Monitoring

The ICC made it clear that, as a prerequisite for its participation in the Global Compact, the Global Compact must not include any form of monitoring. As Maria Livianos Cattaui, then Secretary General of the ICC, put it in an editorial in the *International Herald Tribune*, "Business would look askance at any suggestion involving external assessment of corporate performance, whether by special interest groups or by U.N. agencies."[47] The U.N., for its part, claimed that it had neither the capacity nor the mandate to carry out any sort of monitoring or enforcement of the Global Compact principles.

From the standpoint of public acceptance, the lack of monitoring, while a prerequisite for ICC participation, is perhaps the Global Compact's Achilles' heel. Even NGO supporters of the Compact, such as Amnesty International and Human Rights Watch, have stated that some form of monitoring and sanctions would be necessary. At the inauguration of the Compact, Amnesty's representative said that sanctions for violators and independent monitoring, made publicly available, "are absolutely essential if this initiative is to be effective, credible and win the trust of human rights organizations."[48]

No Logo?

Another highly controversial aspect of the Global Compact is the issue of image. Had the Compact been called the Learning Forum and kept low profile, the issue of bluewash would not have come up. However, the high-profile speech in Davos, the launch in New York and the personal prestige of Kofi Annan have made the Global Compact a high-stakes partnership. From the beginning, the U.N. has been careless about the possibility that corporations would use the Global Compact to wrap themselves in the flag of the United Nations, without committing to actually changing their behavior.

Do the Nike swoosh and the U.N. olive branch really belong together? Is Phil Knight worthy of standing with Kofi Annan for that photo op? Since the Global Compact is neither a monitoring instrument nor a club, that question is not relevant to the Compact managers. However, it is surely relevant to labor rights campaigners, who have targeted Nike for its sweatshop practices. As the case study in Chapter Seven shows, Nike did not keep its promises, either before nor after the Global Compact. Nike's acceptance into the Global Compact network does little for the U.N.'s credibility.

A similar posed picture shows Mr. Annan with a DaimlerChrysler executive; evidently this is the preferred pose for the corporate executives. Understandably so—they get to be associated with the U.N. flag, the symbol of international peace, and with the Nobel Prize–winning Mr. Annan. Nike is a worldwide symbol of sweatshops, and DaimlerChrysler has the largest proportion of gas-guzzling SUVs of any major automaker in the U.S. Mr. Annan is a peacemaker and would like to bring everyone to the table. However, some companies are not ready to be admitted to the world humanitarian community. At the very least, the U.N. has shown poor judgment in allowing Kofi Annan's image to be used in this way.

In addition to Mr. Annan's image, the Global Compact logo—an image that Compact staffperson Georg Kell referred to as "a decomposed globe"—has been used by DaimlerChrysler Corporation in a publication called "The Global Compact." Though the image is missing specific design features that make up the trademarked logo, it is unmistakably similar to the U.N. Global Compact logo. The same image is also used by the International Center for Alcohol Policies (ICAP), which describes itself as a "not-for-profit organization . . . supported by twelve of the world's largest drinks manufacturers."[49] This front for companies like Heineken, Coors, Miller and Molson is listed as a "civil society organization" on the Global Compact website.[50] Outside the Global Compact, the U.N. has shown similar disregard for its own image. A glossy booklet, *The United Nations—The Millennium Summit*, published in New York for the September 2000 Summit, freely mixes ad copy and speeches about world peace, photos of corporate executives and photos of U.N. personnel. This tacky amalgam makes the U.N. Millennium Summit seem like an excuse to sell advertising pages. For those who respect the Secretary General and the U.N., the booklet, which fortunately was not widely distributed, seemed like the precursor of a potential image nightmare for the U.N.[51]

All of this incipient bluewash—this intermingling of U.N. and corporate images—has occurred despite the fact that, simultaneous to the launch of the Global Compact in July 2000, the Secretary General issued a document entitled "Guidelines: Cooperation Between the United Nations and the Business Community."[52] These guidelines provide a general set of rules for how the U.N. should increase its cooperation with corporations "in a manner that ensures the integrity and independence" of the U.N. The forms of cooperation envisioned include advocacy, fundraising, policy dialogue, humanitarian aid and development. Business partners must demonstrate "responsible citizenship"; for-profit enterprises are not "citizens," but the U.N. has accepted this usage.[53]

The guidelines state, "Business entities that are complicit in human rights abuses, tolerate forced or compulsory labor or the use of child labor . . . or that otherwise do not meet the relevant obligations or responsibilities by the United Nations, are not eligible for partnership." This is an example of a guideline that most NGOs would support. However, the U.N. claim that it lacks the capacity to monitor corporations' activities creates a catch-22 situation. How can the world body determine if a corporation is complicit in human rights violations if it cannot monitor its activities? Maybe this is why Mr. Annan appeared to ignore the guidelines just a few days after they were published by inviting Shell to join the Global Compact and its associated partnerships (see Chapter One).

Perhaps the most shocking aspect of the guidelines is that they create the potential to use the U.N. olive-branch emblem on corporate funded projects or partnership projects. Companies may not use the logo to sell their products. But hypothetically, we could see a partnership—a clinic funded by Rio Tinto and operated by WHO, with the Rio Tinto and U.N. logos side by side. For activists fighting Rio Tinto to save their own environment and health, the logo's depiction would be a betrayal. For Rio Tinto it could be a bluewash bonanza—if, for example, it were to publicize this collaboration with the U.N. in a television commercial.

At the launch of the Global Compact, when asked if we might eventually see the Nike swoosh and the U.N. emblem side by side, a Nike representative refused to answer. When asked the next day in a radio interview, she also evaded the question.[54]

The Global Compact in Practice

The first question journalists ask about the Global Compact is, "What companies are in it?" Strangely enough, the answer to this obvious question is, "We don't know." The Global Compact managers have left its membership ambiguous.

At the launch of the Global Compact in July 2000, some fifty companies attended and were counted as Global Compact companies, including biotechnology giants Aventis and Novartis, South African company Eskom, Royal Dutch Shell, BP Amoco, Nike, Unilever and a host of other companies well known for their environmental, labor rights and/or human rights transgressions. An alliance of NGOs, of which CorpWatch was part, was among those that criticized the easy entry of companies into the Compact, saying that the companies were getting to associate with the U.N. without making a commitment to change their behavior (see Appendix C).

Later, perhaps in response to that criticism, the Global Compact Office stopped naming companies that simply signed up, saying that words were not enough—they wanted to see action. Yet the Office naturally wanted to create an impression of success. As of this writing, the Global Compact website still refers to "several hundred"[55] companies that are part of the Global Compact network, but identifies only a few dozen that have sent pilot phase submissions to the Learning Forum. The hundreds of companies have not done enough to be named, but they have done enough to create an impression of momentum. The policy is either secretive or bloated, depending on one's interpretation, but in either case, it is an odd policy for a program touting transparency as one of its tools.[56]

One of the main planks of the Global Compact is the Learning Forum, to which companies must once a year send examples of lessons learned or actions taken. The main advantage of the Global Compact Learning Forum over best practices case studies published by the WBCSD or ICC is that the Global Compact will have an academic committee evaluate the studies before publication. Using this advantage, the U.N. could create a learning forum that governments and communities would trust, as opposed to the self-serving case studies of business associations. With serious evaluation, the Global Compact could be considered an improvement over business-only initiatives.

Independent evaluation, while important, also revealed the weakness of the early corporate contributions. The Global Compact Office was slated to web-publish its first set of corporate case studies in July 2001, on the one-year anniversary of its launch. In July, the office announced that the case studies would be delayed until the first Learning Forum, which took place in London in October 2001. At that Learning Forum, U.N. officials discovered that "none of the company submissions conformed to the case study guidelines suggested by the Global Compact Office," and about half "did not make reference to any of the nine GC principles."[57]

Nearly two years after its launch, the Global Compact has not published a single case study. Instead, by mid-2002, it had posted only what it calls "pilot phase submissions" or "examples." Forty-four of these were published on the Global Compact website and included several recycled items—examples of corporate "best practices" from before the Global Compact was launched. In keeping with the best practices tradition, many chronicled trivial actions. There was a heavy emphasis on management system achievements, rather than steps that resulted in a change noticeable to the outside world. Essentially, these examples amount to reporting that the corporate orchestra has tuned up, and the conductor found the baton. The symphony has not yet been played.

The failure of even the highest-profile Global Compact companies, like Eskom, Shell and Novartis, to post presentable case studies to the Global Compact office also provokes one to wonder how many ICC and WBCSD case studies would have been published had there been an independent review. As the U.N. Research Institute for Social Development (UNRISD) points out, a handful of anecdotes provide the "evidence" for a supposed "paradigm shift" in business attitudes and practices. UNRISD views progress on corporate responsibility through voluntary Codes of Conduct and other voluntary initiatives as "incipient and piecemeal."[58] Even the architects of the Global Compact acknowledge that the fact that the Global Compact recognizes and promotes "a company's 'good practices' provides no guarantee that the same company does not and will not engage in 'bad' ones elsewhere."[59]

Though it sounds terrific, "best practices," as promoted by business at the U.N., may not be of that much help after all. Taken as a whole, best practice case studies and their promotion are meant to convey the message that business understands the problems and is already finding solutions, and governments need not meddle in this process of innovation. So-called best practice case studies can be a diversion from the need for corporate accountability.

Big Business in Johannesburg

While Rio set the stage for controversial corporate collaborations, the intervening decade established corporate partnerships as the U.N.'s new modus operandi vis-à-vis the private sector. As a result, the Johannesburg Earth Summit became even more business-friendly than the Rio Summit. In Johannesburg, big business gained an even deeper foothold into global governance through partnership with the U.N. Moreover, the corporate partnerships were lauded as the major outcome of Johannesburg, even though they are voluntary, vague and piecemeal.

As discussed in Chapter Two, the WBCSD was formed specifically to advise Maurice Strong and the Rio Summit on business's role in sustainable development. It has remained active since. For Johannesburg, the WBCSD joined with the ICC to form yet another grouping, Business Action for Sustainable Development (BASD), which was designed to be the main business voice for the Johannesburg Summit. Their message: "business is part of the solution." BASD was straightforward about its goal of ensuring "the world business community is assigned its proper place in preparations for the Summit, and that we are seen at the event itself to be playing a constructive role."[60]

According to Corporate Europe Observatory, at the first meeting of the BASD, in Paris, on October 4, 2001, it was clear that the main political goals of the group revolved around avoiding new regulations and promoting voluntary measures and "self-regulation." These goals were openly stated by the Chair and by the U.S. Council for International Business representative. In addition, BASD appeared concerned with sidestepping NGO criticism. The centerpiece of its promotional agenda was a series of anecdotal case studies on "How Business Contributes to Sustainable Development," similar to the approach of the WBCSD and the Global Compact.[61]

The BASD did not object to the presence of controversial companies. For instance, Rio Tinto and BP are among the members with checkered recent histories. TotalFinaElf is a BASD participant, despite its business partnership with the brutal Burmese military regime and the association of its pipeline project there with crimes against humanity, including forced labor and forced relocation.[62]

The role of Shell is the clearest signal of BASD's approach. As discussed in Chapter One, Mark Moody Stuart, until recently the head of Shell, is the chair of the BASD. Another Shell executive, Phillip Watts, is the chairman of the WBCSD, adding to Shell's elite role among corporate environmentalists. As head of Shell, Moody Stuart had enormous experience with the tribulations—and trials—of corporations under fire; he had to deal with the aftermath of the Brent Spar scandal in Europe and the execution of Ken Saro-Wiwa and his Ogoni comrades in Nigeria. Shell's role is surely both symbolic and significant in the world of corporate responsibility and corporate greenwash. The choice of Shell's chief for the head of BASD certainly did not bode well for citizen campaigners pushing the Johannesburg Summit to take on corporate accountability.

In the lead-up to Johannesburg, some European countries attempted to include references to the Global Compact in the

Summit documents, and NGOs counterattempted to include references to corporate accountability. The crux of the matter was that governments had little to no hope of negotiating multilateral agreements and shied away from any serious attempts. They were left with restating some of Agenda 21, although, sadly, the language tended to be weaker than the language of ten years earlier, reflecting how Marrakech had indeed trumped Rio.

To salvage Earth Summit II, the U.N. came up with the idea of partnerships for implementation. In U.N.-speak, these were known as "Type Two" outcomes, as opposed to "Type One" outcomes, which were traditional, negotiated, multilateral agreements. On the one hand, the partnership approach had some advantages: Countries could avoid the lowest-common-denominator language that plagues U.N. accords. They could select partners from other countries and sectors. They might get some financial resources from the private sector. Perhaps most significantly, they could exclude the United States, which would eliminate the single biggest obstacle to progress on international environmental issues.

On the other hand, it's not clear the Type Two partnerships will accomplish anything beneficial. Some partnerships, like one spearheaded by Habitat for Humanity, seem quite positive. Others, involving the biotech industry, for example, seem a classic exercise in engineering consent for genetically engineered foods and gaining market access for Western multinationals.

In Johannesburg, the world's governments found themselves incapable of recommitting to the environment and to development at the same level as they had at Rio. Ideologically and politically, in a decade, the world had moved backward on sustainable development. If the public had seen this clearly, they might have realized that it would have been better to cancel the Conference altogether.

The Type Two partnerships, touted as innovative and flexible, were to be the saviors of the Summit. In order to promote this kind of outcome, corporations had to be invited into the system and given a central place in the outcome of the Summit. This was reflected in the physical arrangements in Johannesburg, which allowed business a conference center near the official meeting venue while keeping most NGOs and potential protestors miles away from government delegates and ministers. UNEP—the same U.N. agency that had identified the growing gap between corporate practice and sustainable development (as we saw in Chapter One)—rewarded businesses with World Summit Business Awards for Sustainable Development Partnerships, issued jointly with the ICC and given during the Johannesburg meeting.[63] It was a sad day for UNEP, and for the U.N.

CHAPTER FOUR

Corporate Accountability in the Twenty-First Century

On the morning of November 30, 1999, as the Ministerial meeting of the WTO was scheduled to begin in Seattle, Kofi Annan was stuck in his hotel. Like most delegates to the meeting, he was unable to get to the conference center due to the tactically brilliant nonviolent street blockades formed by affinity groups of protestors. Through the tear gas, Mr. Annan must have seen firsthand the determination of the militant wing of the anticorporate globalization movement, and presumably he had time to contemplate the meaning and power of this historic act of civil disobedience. Certainly, he must have been hoping the U.N. would never become a target of this movement. At the Millennium Summit nearly a year later, Mr. Annan seemed relieved that hundreds of NGO representatives were inside the U.N., willing to listen and engage, rather than outside protesting.

There was also a protest against corporatization of the U.N. at the Millennium Summit, but it was small enough to go unnoticed by the Secretary General. It was small in part because the heavy influence of the corporate lobby on the U.N. left the movement for global justice in an awkward position. On the one hand, a central tenet of the movement was that the WTO has too much power and must be reined in, if not abolished. The logical institution to counterbalance the WTO, in theory the most democratic of the global intergovernmental institutions, is the U.N. If peace, human rights and sustainability are our highest values, then the U.N. should hold a place at the very apex of global governance. In theory, pro-U.N. demonstrations are the only kind one would see—outside of right wing U.S. circles. On the other hand, if the U.N. becomes as beholden to corporate interests as the WTO, the equation could certainly change. Many citizen movements would lose interest in fighting for an increased U.N. role in global politics. In fact, the U.N. has come perilously close to losing broad chunks of people's movements already. At the Fourth PrepCom (preparatory meeting) in Bali, there were calls to boycott PrepCom by the Indonesian People's Forum. South African groups were bitterly divided over whether to protest at Johannesburg or not. Even some groups that have invested a lot of effort into the Johannesburg process have contemplated giving up.

The U.N. also finds itself in a bind. Officials are nervous that in the age of globalization, the world body will become irrelevant if it does not embrace the realpolitik of corporate power. Yet they also realize the danger of some of their staunchest supporters turning on them if the U.N. continues to open its doors to the corporate globalization agenda. Should the U.N. become too closely associated with such a corporate agenda, global justice protests could begin to target the U.N., as they have targeted the G-8, the WTO and the World Bank. The state of play going into the Johannesburg Summit left the global justice movement ambivalent as to whether to protest in favor of or against the United Nations.

Marching to Johannesburg

In intergovernmental environmental negotiations since Rio, it has been the United States, Canada and Australia that have most often thwarted effective multilateral agreements.[1] The backdrop to this problem is the ongoing hold that corporations have on U.S. environmental policymaking and the related prioritization by the U.S. and its closest allies of the globalization project. A great deal of the positive energy from citizen movements that went into Rio was thwarted by the rise of corporate globalization. The U.N. was a marginal institution for the globalization process, which is no doubt where the U.S. preferred to keep it.

When the anti-corporate globalization movement burst on the scene in Seattle in late 1999, the most publicized elements were organized labor and the militant, mostly young, street blockaders. However, there was another faction critical of the WTO in Seattle, one that included internationally oriented NGOs, such as the environmental and developmental groups that had attended Rio with such high hopes in 1992. This faction included a few clairvoyant critics, such as Vandana Shiva, Martin Khor and Ralph Nader, who had essentially predicted the showdown over corporate globalization as early as Rio and had helped frame much of the critique of the WTO and other trade accords. These groups were an important part of the mix in subsequent demonstrations in Washington, Prague, Quebec, Genoa and Porto Alegre. Their support for strong governmental and intergovernmental regulation of corporations was, in many cases, overshadowed by a more general anticorporate message, including the antistate views of anarchists.

A great deal of the mainstream media focused on the diversity of the movement, frequently ridiculing it for variations in policy among its various wings. For example, many protestors in Seattle were advocating for environmental and labor side agreements to be part of the WTO, while others felt these agreements should be kept out of the WTO. The latter group believed environmental and labor standards should be housed in U.N.-brokered multilateral agreements, with which trade and investment rules would have to comply. The spirit of both groups' policies is similar: a higher priority for labor and environmental protections and a lower one for trade and investment rules; the immediate policy recommendations vary.

For all the ideological diversity in what is known as the Seattle, or anti–corporate globalization, movement, virtually all wings agree on one fundamental thing: Corporations have too much power. The corollary belief is that we desperately need better corporate accountability mechanisms—greater democratic control over corporations—if we are ever going to get the world on a path of basic fairness, sustainability and democracy. The U.N. must embrace corporate accountability if it is to maintain widespread support of citizen movements. The U.N. must advocate for international regulation of corporate behavior in the environmental, human rights and labor rights realms if it is going to be truly relevant in the age of globalization—if it is going to be more than a baby brother to the WTO. However, such an approach would put the U.N. at odds with its most powerful member states and governments, such as the U.S., which have already clearly demonstrated their propensity for economic blackmail when they disagree with the direction the U.N. is taking.

This conundrum was in full view in the lead-up to Johannesburg, where the global justice movement remained in limbo. Some wanted to protest the U.N., some to support the governments, some to protest only industry's role. Many were hoping for a more effective, democratic and powerful U.N., but were unable to throw their weight behind any institution so aligned with the corporate agenda. In Johannesburg, the U.N. followed the ideological trail it had embarked upon in Rio and had continued to blaze throughout the ensuing decade. It also pleased its funders, especially the U.S., as it embraced an ineffectual concept of voluntary corporate responsibility, instead of advocating for corporate accountability.

Accountability vs. Responsibility

There is a great deal of confusion around the terms "corporate responsibility" and "corporate accountability." *Corporate responsibility* refers to voluntary measures for environmentally and socially beneficial behavior, while *corporate accountability* refers to holding companies to societal norms or having them face consequences. Examples of corporate responsibility would include a company eliminating child labor, improving working conditions or reducing toxic waste emissions on its own. The motivation for the new behavior might be cost savings, improved reputation or simply that the managers thought it the ethical thing to do. Commonly, corporate responsibility advocates emphasize the "business argument," meaning that corporate responsibility is also good for the bottom line. The financial benefit can be from savings on direct costs, avoiding bad publicity and boycotts or finding a niche market for a product perceived as socially beneficial by a sufficient number of customers.

A major component of the corporate responsibility approach—one which has clearly manifested itself at both Earth Summits as well as in Kofi Annan's treatment of the issue—is that of promoting dialogue between corporations and activist groups. But while this is often a good PR strategy for a company, its results in terms of truly changing corporate behavior are questionable. As *Petroleum Intelligence Weekly* observes, "Both Big Oil and the NGOs now talk in terms of dialogue rather than confrontation, but what has it achieved? Mostly, oil companies now recognize the need to improve communication and consultation—hence the mountain of material now produced on social and environmental performance. But what it hasn't done is lead to concrete changes in company policy."[2]

As we have seen throughout this book, corporate responsibility is the approach advocated by the WBCSD, the ICC, the BASD and the Global Compact. Yet it is important to underscore that corporations themselves regularly acknowledge that promotion of corporate responsibility in environment, human rights, poverty alleviation and community service is, at least in part, a tactic aimed at avoiding accountability measures—that is, legislation and regulation of corporate behavior.

An example of corporate accountability would be if a company causing harm or breaking the law is sued and forced to pay a fine or

forced to change the illegal behavior. Another example of accountability is the requirement of reporting toxic emissions. Under U.S. law,
for example, companies are required literally to "account" for their
emissions. A third example would be a group of corporations, such as
the manufacturers of ozone-depleting chemicals like CFCs or methyl
bromide, being forced by an international U.N.-brokered accord to
phase out these harmful chemicals. A fourth example is when a company is forced to alter its behavior or pushed out of a certain line of
business by a consumer or investment boycott. In this last example,
the accountability is not to the government, but to consumers and
investors. The line between "responsibility" (the company chooses to
do the right thing) and "accountability" (the company is forced to do
the right thing because it will lose money if it does not) is slightly
blurred in this last case, but the essential difference is still clear: the
company is being held accountable for its actions.

A major limitation of the corporate responsibility "movement," as
it is sometimes known, is that the definition of responsible behavior is
usually left to the company itself. In a few cases, independent bodies
like the Global Reporting Initiative are set up to evaluate reporting by
companies, but the reporting itself is voluntary. When corporate
responsibility is not good for the bottom line, there is no recourse for
government or citizens. For example, at the Ford Motor Company's
annual shareholder meeting in 2000, Chairman William Ford
acknowledged that SUVs were unsafe and bad for the environment.
But, he said, the company would have to continue making them in
order to compete with GM and Chrysler. Still, many environmentalists welcomed the admission, thinking it would lead eventually to an
emphasis on more fuel-efficient cars. However, two years later, Ford
was still lobbying against better fuel-efficiency standards and had
backed off its green rhetoric and promises.[3] Under current rules and
power relations, Ford cannot be held to account for this failure of
responsibility.

That a large company like Ford with an environmentalist CEO is
not able to tackle voluntarily one of the most significant environmental issues in the world is surely a sign that corporate responsibility is
not enough, that accountability through regulation is a minimum
necessity. Yet new regulation is routinely derided as old-fashioned,
inefficient, command-and-control and antimarket.

Another example of the severe limitations of corporate responsibility is the Swiss engineering giant Asea Brown and Bovari (ABB).
ABB executives were central in the formation of the WBCSD and the
theories of "eco-efficiency" promoted at the Rio Summit. Yet its CEO
through much of the 1990s, Percy Barnevik, said, "I would define

globalisation as the freedom for my group of companies to invest where it wants when it wants, to produce what it wants, to buy and sell where it wants, and support the fewest restrictions possible coming from labour laws and social conventions."[4] Barnevik was known as the Jack Welch of Europe, for his tough approach to cost cutting and job cutting. Barnevik's successor, Goran Lindahl, was appointed by Kofi Annan as a special consultant to the Global Compact. An executive with a reputation for a progressive, ethical outlook, he theoretically had the credibility to recruit other major companies into the Compact that would soften the hard edges of Barnevik's vision of globalization. But a year after his UN appointment, Lindahl (along with Barnevik) was at the center of a scandal involving a bloated retirement package that came in the same year that ABB posted a $690 million loss.[5] Throughout this time, ABB promoted itself as a corporate responsibility leader within the business world. But that did not inoculate its own leaders from greed.

Often, the very same corporations promoting themselves as responsible are actively working to prevent measures for corporate accountability, such as international treaties and conventions, transnational lawsuits, national legislation, personal liability and so on. Companies lobbying against and evading accountability should not be considered "responsible." Corporate pledges of responsibility to communities, governments or the United Nations must not be taken at face value, but rather monitored.

Toward Global Accountability

The essence of the global justice movement consists of values that demand that the current corporate-globalization paradigm, which prioritizes corporate profit maximization over human rights, labor rights and environmental rights, be turned on its head. This core belief is wholly consistent with the charter and purpose of the United Nations. Another central belief of the Seattle movement is that corporations have gained so much power in the realms of finance, culture and politics that democracy itself is under attack. The U.N. would also like to bring business in line with the universal values; however, it has little leverage to do so, as its most powerful Member States have chosen to give more power to the WTO. Given this dilemma, the U.N. has decided to try to persuade and cajole business into its orbit.

Thus, we find ourselves where we are today: with Earth Summit documents that emphasize corporate responsibility measures, rather than a binding legal framework for corporate accountability. In fact, during the negotiations leading up to Johannesburg, corporate responsibility and accountability were conflated in draft documents. A Friends of the Earth proposal for a Corporate Accountability Convention was deemed a "terrible idea" by a U.S. State Department official and never made it to the table,[6] though watered down references to corporate accountability appeared in, disappeared from and reappeared in Johannesburg text drafts.

At the same time, forces within the United Nations are sympathetic to calls for greater corporate accountability. Powerful social forces—forces that are gathering strength again following a pause after September 11, 2001, and in the wake of the collapse of the Enron corporation—will bring pressure on the Member States and on the U.N. agencies to take the need for corporate accountability more seriously in the near future.

The rest of this chapter consists of suggestions for steps, some theoretical and some practical, for moving the U.N., its Member States and "we the peoples" toward a corporate accountability framework for sustainability and global justice.

Redefine Sustainability

As discussed in Chapter One, one of the key weaknesses of Rio was the failure to define terms like "sustainable," "development" and "sustainable development," allowing all actors to define these terms to their liking. For example, one meaning of "development" is economic growth. "Sustainable" can be taken to mean the growth will continue. "Sustainable development," therefore, would mean ongoing economic growth. In the Earth Summit context, this rather unecological meaning is justified by the argument that poor countries need growth and jobs in order to reduce poverty and that the accompanying environmental and social problems are simply sacrifices that must be made. With these definitions, the link between "sustainable" and "development"—what German writer Wolfgang Sachs presciently called a "dangerous liaison" in 1991—does more harm than good.[7]

In a more encouraging definition, "sustainable" can refer to the pace or nature of an activity such that the activity does not deplete or pollute natural resources faster than they can recover. "Development" could mean economic activities democratically chosen by any people with self-determination and access to information. "Sustainable development" would, therefore, mean democratically chosen economic activities that do not compromise the ecological basis for the future. In this definition, the link between "sustainable" and "development" is an important conceptual one.

An important step in the redefinition of sustainability is the realization that the industrialized world has not discovered it. When Indira Gandhi said, "Poverty is the worst polluter,"[8] she surely did not intend to let overconsumption of resources off the hook. She probably did not imagine it would be used by the mining industry, to name one example, to justify the need for mining subsidies in the United States.[9] The Californian driving an SUV, filling a swimming pool with fresh water, buying pesticide-laden fruit flown in fresh from South America, eating beef from hormone-pumped cattle and using ten times the energy of a Bangladeshi, is not a more sustainable citizen than the landless Brazilian peasant cutting down forest to grow crops to feed his or her family.

On a global scale, wealth is a worse polluter than poverty, although poverty certainly causes enormous local environmental catastrophes and other forms of misery. A rediscovered definition of "sustainability" must recognize the inherent unsustainability of both poverty and excessive wealth, as well as the inherently socially unsustainable nature of vast inequalities in wealth distribution.

Separate Corporations and the State

Complicating any attempt to confront corporate power is the widespread support for the status quo among governments. Few governments deviate from accepting a basic dynamic of competition to attract investment to create jobs and wealth. At the U.N., business's claim of representing "a part of the solution" to environment and development problems is accepted by the Secretary General and most delegations. The trend toward privatization is virtually worldwide. Political influence by corporations on governments is also widely accepted. The forms of this influence include legal campaign contributions (U.S.), direct representation in government (Italy) and corruption (Mexico).

At the same time, the global justice movement, which is broadly supportive of the U.N., has identified "corporate-led globalization," and corporate power in general, as one of the main battlegrounds in its struggles. Therefore, the movement against excessive corporate power is also a movement to expose its corrupting influence on governments and intergovernmental bodies—in other words, a movement to strengthen democracy locally, nationally and internationally.

There must be a separation of corporations and the state. Just as the intertwinement of religion and the state can lead to a religious fundamentalist state antithetical to democracy, so can the intertwinement of corporations and the state lead to a corporate fundamentalist (or market fundamentalist) state, also antithetical to democracy. Separation of corporations and the state should also extend from local and national governance, to global governance institutions, such as the WTO, World Bank, IMF, U.N., etc.

One key component of this effort would be long-term campaigns to eliminate the phenomenon of state subsidies for corporations, known as "corporate welfare," as well as special corporate rights and corporate access to power through lobbying and campaign contributions.

Dialogue vs. Confrontation

Multi-stakeholder dialogues, partnerships and similar processes are in vogue, as is the concept of satisfying all stakeholders in general. Kofi Annan joined the stampede when, in a message sent from New York during the World Economic Forum, he scolded the World Social Forum participants in Brazil, "You in civil society must show that you are ready to work in partnerships for change, rather than remain aloof through the politics of confrontation."[10] The message implied that partnership is the only way forward; confrontation—even nonviolent confrontation—is never productive.

Yet that is not the experience of many environmental and developmental groups. Many are still "engaged" in confrontation and direct action on corporations, not because they are behind-the-times throwbacks to the 1970s, but because it works, at least on occasion. In many campaigns, negotiation with adversaries, corporate or governmental, is inevitable. As Martin Luther King, Jr. wrote in his 1963 "Letter from a Birmingham Jail," negotiation is the purpose of direct action. Confrontations aim to create enough power and tension to force the powerful to negotiate and to achieve results from the negotiations.

However, at the U.N. these days, as well as in other forums, being part of the solution is almost a requirement for acquiring permission to speak. Criticism of corporate misbehavior is considered negative and unproductive. Solutions, dialogue and partnerships are mature; negativity is forbidden. Without doubt, a focus on solutions is attractive. Who does not want to be part of the solution? If corporations have overwhelming power, it is tempting to believe that they, too, are ready to be part of the solution. In fact it is necessary that they join in finding solutions. The BASD, to name just one business grouping, aims to deliver this exact message, that business is part of the solution to environmental and development problems.

Yet this approach ignores some fundamental realities. First, it is impossible to find solutions when there is still disagreement on the source of the problem. Business has been claiming itself part of the solution since Rio, but solutions beyond rhetoric and best practices case studies have failed to materialize as the crises of environment and development have deepened—or worse still, its solutions have in fact exacerbated the problems. Second, the pressure for dialogue and against confrontation, overwhelming though it might be, is not designed to increase citizen leverage, but often gives the most powerful forces at the table the upper hand. Third, to the extent that corporations have embraced corporate responsibility, it is largely because of so-called negative campaigning, also known as pressure campaigning. Shell, probably the world's leading giant company in self-proclaimed commitment to environmental and social goals, took this role on after the Brent Spar and Nigeria scandals. The intensely negative attacks from civil society drove Shell to change its rhetoric, if not its behavior.

Orwellian though it sounds, when it comes to corporate campaigning, negative is positive. Pressure campaigns may be unpleasant and hurt some people's feelings, but there are no case studies of pressure campaigns causing a company to pollute more or violate human rights more frequently. Sometimes they result in healthy changes, even if those changes are made reluctantly. The one truly negative outcome of campaigns for better standards, especially higher wages, is the threat that a company will cut and run, a reality that speaks to the need, as economic globalization proceeds, for corporate accountability campaigners to improve their capacity for international advocacy efforts. These efforts can include traditional solidarity campaigns in which activists in the home country of a corporation expose that firm's behavior in another country. They can also extend to more strategically integrated international campaigns against single companies or entire sectors.

The simple fact that corporations have global webs forces citizen movements to create equally global webs. We have seen such webs emerge and become increasingly effective when confronting institutions such as the WTO or the World Bank. The successful campaign against the Multilateral Agreement on Investment was an excellent example.[11] Some transnational campaigns, such as the global effort to hold Nestlé and other infant formula manufacturers accountable in the 1970s, which resulted in the WHO code of conduct, are an important part of the history of corporate campaigning and should be studied. Cooperation between the Ogoni and European and North American supporters, or between South American indigenous people and human rights organizations on all continents, are some of the most exciting corporate accountability work in the world today.

The U.N. and Global Corporate Accountability

Some international corporate accountability initiatives don't necessarily define themselves as such; rather they focus on forging international treaties, such as the ones on the ozone layer, tobacco, persistent organic pollutants, biodiversity and climate change. While corporations and their industry associations continue to lobby aggressively to weaken international agreements, these key mechanisms can be used to hold transnational corporations accountable on a global scale. As discussed in Chapter Three, these U.N.-brokered agreements are key battlefields in the struggle for global corporate accountability.

International treaties and conventions are created by governments, and business should be kept out of the process. Because corporations are at the root of the problems they address, these accords—despite weak enforcement mechanisms as compared to institutions such as the WTO—can provide binding frameworks for empowering governments to subordinate transnational corporations to universal values such as environmental rights. The more successful of these efforts tend to combine local, national and global organization to create pressure for strong international rules.

Within the U.N. system, other structures and important individuals can be allies in the movement for corporate accountability. One of these structures is the Sub-Commission on the Promotion and Protection of Human Rights, composed of twenty-six independent members and the main subsidiary body of the U.N. Commission on Human Rights. In the year 2000, the Sub-Commission issued a report looking at globalization through the prism of human rights, calling the WTO a "nightmare" for developing countries and recommending that the trade body be brought under the U.N.'s purview.[12] In contrast to the Secretary General's belief that the multilateral trade regime is the success story of the century, the report calls for a "radical review of the whole system of trade liberalization."[13]

The Sub-Commission has a Working Group on transnational corporations and human rights. This Working Group decided at its 1999 session to draft a Code of Conduct on corporations and human rights. The Code was approved for further development at the 2000 and 2001 meetings. The document made it clear that the Code might eventually be viewed as legally binding and that provisions for monitoring and compliance would be integrated into the Code.[14] Unfortunately, but predictably, the U.S. opposes this foray into the topic of human rights and corporations, and has called on the U.N. to eliminate the Sub-Commission entirely, backing proposals that would drastically curtail its capacity.[15] Despite the long-shot odds against it, and despite its relative isolation on these issues in the constellation of

U.N. agencies and commissions, the Sub-Commission provides a beacon of hope for continuing to build an approach that specifically aims to hold corporations accountable.

In the preparatory meetings for Earth Summit II, the environmental group Friends of the Earth International proposed a Framework Convention on Corporate Accountability. Though it received scant support from governments, it lays out a vision for achieving a measure of democratic control over superpowerful global corporations at the international level.

The Convention proposal contains the following elements:

- Corporate reporting requirements on environmental and social impacts
- Prior consultation with affected communities, including environmental impact assessments and access to information
- Extended liability to directors for corporate breaches of environmental and social laws; corporate liability for breaches of international laws or agreements
- Rights of redress for citizens, including access for affected people anywhere in the world to pursue litigation when corporations are listed, a provision for legal challenge to company decisions by stakeholders, and a legal aid mechanism to provide public funds to support such challenges
- Community rights to resources, including indigenous people's rights over common property, such as forest, fisheries and minerals
- Veto rights over developmental projects and against displacement; a right to compensation for resources expropriated by corporations
- Sanctions against companies breaching these duties, for example, suspending stock exchange listing, fines and (in extreme cases) de-chartering or withdrawal of limited liability status

What if the Third Earth Summit in 2012 shed its business-friendly frills and made corporate accountability for the environment its central theme? What if U.N. agencies were given the mandate to figure out corporate accountability mechanisms, instead of forging flimsy partnerships with the private sector? What if U.N. Secretary General Kofi Annan, in his second and last term, were to put his prestige and influence behind an initiative such as an accountability convention—one that goes beyond the minor ambitions of the "learning forums," "best practices case studies" and "participatory platforms" that make up the Global Compact?

The cynical answer is "he would lose his job." But the answer may well be that if the Secretary General of the United Nation led the world in creating such a global accord, we might actually make some significant steps to flipping the dominant paradigm on its head and subordinating the corporate drive for profits to the imperatives of labor, environmental and human rights. This, in turn, might transform the globalization dynamic from a corporate-driven one, to one driven by "we the peoples."

Alliance for a Corporate-Free U.N.

There is a global activist initiative to try to turn the U.N. around on these issues. The Alliance for a Corporate-Free U.N. is an international network of human rights, environmental and development groups working to address undue corporate influence in the United Nations and to support U.N. initiatives holding corporations accountable on issues of human rights, labor rights and the environment. The members of the Alliance believe in a U.N. that holds commercial rules subservient to human rights, labor and environmental principles, that avoids excessive and undue corporate influence, that holds corporations accountable in a legal framework, that maintains the integrity of international social and environmental agreements and that receives adequate funding from governments.[16]

The Alliance has worked on three main activities: it has monitored and exposed corporate partnerships and undue corporate influence at the U.N.; it has taken action to pressure the U.N. to avoid such partnerships and influence by speaking out through the media, dialoguing with U.N. officials and lobbying governments at various U.N. forums; and it works to promote and support U.N.-related measures to hold corporations accountable, such as those discussed above. The Alliance has also drafted an alternative to the Global Compact, called the Citizens Compact. Endorsed by more than seventy human rights and environmental groups from around the world, the Citizens Compact lays out a foundation for cooperation between the U.N. and nonbusiness, nongovernmental groups to work for the proper relationships between the U.N. and business. The Citizens Compact emphasizes the need for monitoring and the enforcement of a legal framework for corporate behavior (see Appendix B).

Countering Corporate Globalization

At present, corporations are legally accountable to their stockholders, but only voluntarily responsible to many so-called stakeholders. The United Nations must play a central role in making transnational companies accountable to workers, governments, citizens, consumers, intergovernmental organizations, neighbors and hosts, as well as to stockholders. The U.N. is still the only global organization that can potentially serve as a counterbalance to corporate-driven globalization and the institutions that propel it, including the WTO, the World Bank and the IMF.

Globalization means that communities, workers, consumers and others around the world are feeling the effects of the growing power and reach of transnational corporations every day. Many are fighting back, organizing for justice locally. Some are working on the national level in their countries; some are increasingly recognizing the need to work internationally—and in fact globally—to counter corporate-driven globalization. These constituencies, which make up "we the peoples," need the United Nations to be on their side. They need the U.N. to do what it is supposed to do—stand up for their human rights, their rights to good health, to live in a clean environment, to organize in the workplace. They need the U.N. to hold corporations accountable.

In this context, the trend toward U.N.-corporate partnerships is not helpful. The financial and political influence of corporations at the United Nations must be greatly diminished. The U.N.'s capacity to serve as the global institution that exerts democratic control over corporations must be bolstered. The world desperately needs the U.N. to boldly step out onto the playing field and set the rules of the game, rather than sitting on the sidelines, leading cheers for corporate responsibility.

At Earth Summit I in Rio, environmentalists accused governments of selling out the planet. At the Kyoto Protocol negotiations at The Hague, climate-protection groups said the Climate Convention was turning into a trade fair. At Earth Summit II in Johannesburg, U.N.-corporate partnerships threatened to turn the planet into a business theme park. For the past decade, the U.N. has listened to the voice of business and industry. It is time for the U.N. to pay closer attention to citizen movements for corporate accountability.

PART TWO

Rhetoric and Reality

CHAPTER · FIVE

One Wash, Two Wash, Greenwash, Bluewash

In Part I of this book, we attempted to explain how business has gained undue influence at both Earth Summits and in the United Nations, documenting how partnership has become the relationship of choice between the U.N. and the private sector. In Part II, we will provide evidence that this relationship is bad for sustainable development and for the U.N.

The short examples in the following chapters are of two kinds. The first, "greenwash snapshots," looks at ten companies' advertising claims relating to environment and health issues and compares their rhetoric with the reality.[1] Taken as a whole, this body of evidence demonstrates that the environmental advertising emanating from the big corporate polluters, while high-quality in public relations terms, casts a thin, green veil over these corporations' true environmental impacts. Any belief that business has the problem under control, that the rest of us can relax because business is part of the solution, is unwarranted. Vigilance and pressure on corporate behavior are required, now as much as ever.

Classic Greenwash

Classic greenwash usually means environmental image advertising. Pristine natural scenery and pious declarations of respect for the earth are the greenwash clichés we have seen many times from mining, nuclear and chemical giants, among others. The aim is simple: to promote a clean and green corporate image.

Deep Greenwash

At the Rio Earth Summit, greenwash went global, with a strategic attempt to portray not only individual corporations, but also business and industry as allies in the struggle to save the planet. Since these allies purportedly understood the world's problems and were working to solve them, no new regulations or monitoring programs would be necessary. Deep greenwash refers to the political effort to avoid democratic control of corporate behavior through a combination of PR and lobbying muscle.

Greenwash / Bluewash

Greenwash (n.): 1. Disinformation disseminated by an organization so as to present an environmentally responsible public image (*Tenth Edition of the Concise Oxford English Dictionary*); 2. The phenomenon of socially and environmentally destructive corporations attempting to preserve and expand their markets by posing as friends of the environment and leaders in the struggle to eradicate poverty (CorpWatch).

Bluewash (n.): 1. The flagrant misuse of the social and human rights legitimacy of the United Nations by corporations who do not in fact adhere to the core principles of the various U.N. declarations (Friends of the Earth); 2. Efforts by corporations to be perceived as part of the world humanitarian community through voluntary associations with the United Nations, without provisions for accountability (CorpWatch).

Bluewash

The second type of example in part two is of companies that have endorsed the Global Compact, but that (in our judgment) have violated one or more of its principles since the Global Compact's launch. Although the U.N. insists that it cannot and does not wish to monitor corporate compliance with the Principles, common sense indicates that a declaration of support for Global Compact principles means that a company is pledging to adhere to them. Ignoring those principles makes a mockery of the U.N. and the concept of partnership. These examples do not represent a complete inventory of Global Compact violations, even for the companies studied, but rather a small sampling of what the U.N. might find if it were to monitor the hundreds of corporations it says have joined the Global Compact.[2] Because the principles are vague and the UN has not provided methods for evaluating compliance, our assertion of Compact violations is based on our understanding of those principles, which are contained in Appendix A.

Though it is discouraging and "negative" to say so, the evidence is that despite all the rhetoric, the global business community does not understand, and is not committed to, sustainable development. By sustainable development, we mean democratically taken decisions about economic activity that do not compromise the health of the planet for the future.

CHAPTER SIX

Greenwash Snapshots

You've seen the ads: Lush green forests. Stunning birds of prey in flight. Humpback whales breaching. Pristine streams glimmering in the sunlight. Inspiringly diverse workers and community children enjoying life to the fullest. All photographed beautifully and reproduced at great expense.

But something is a little off. Somewhere on the page, sometime on the screen, you see the tagline: *At Fossil Fuels Are Us, Inc., We Care.*

Ever since the environmental movement got serious at the first Earth Day, some of the biggest polluters and biodiversity destroyers have been telling us, in pious tones, how much they care about the earth, how they would never do anything to harm it. The world's most polluting corporations have developed some sophisticated techniques to communicate a message of corporate environmentalism, complementing these techniques with an equally sophisticated campaign to ensure governmental and intergovernmental actions do not interfere with business. The first part of this book documented how successful that campaign has been at the United Nations.

If business were really on a path to sustainability, success would be welcomed. But looking at the reality of business behavior instead of the rhetoric tells us this is simply not the case. The promises of the first generation of greenwash have been broken, and greenwash has become even more sophisticated since it was invented. The case studies in this chapter show that the gap between rhetoric and reality remains wide. The past may have been a problem, goes the rhetoric, but now we have seen the light. "We didn't do anything wrong, and we'll never do it again"—this was the message ten years ago, at the first Earth Summit, and it is still the message today. Corporate influence on the U.N. is indeed a serious problem, because the reality remains that big business, while it may be part of the solution in the future, is mostly a part of the problem in the present. There are at least five common forms of greenwash. Here are some techniques companies use to greenwash their image:

Seduce You with Image Ads

The simplest form of greenwash is the environmental image advertisement. Here a company name, like Phillips Petroleum, or a product, such as a gas-guzzling SUV, is placed in a gorgeous natural setting. No specific environmental claims are made, but the advertisers hope the feel will rub off on the consumer, a subconscious association of their company with natural beauty. If natural beauty has nothing to with the company's products, it's greenwash.

Impress You with Tangential Projects

Here the company gets more specific. They talk about the acres of wetlands they've preserved, the studies of biodiversity they have funded and the endangered species that roost on their properties. However, when you research the projects in question, you find they are sometimes forced upon the company by regulators due to past violations, and only later presented as voluntary. Sometimes the ads publicizing the project cost more than the project itself. That's greenwash.

Distract You from Their Destructive Products

Sometimes a company will call attention to its improving safety record, its reduction in polluting emissions, or its energy-efficient factories. These are all fine, if true, but do not address the destructiveness of the company's core business itself. In analyzing a company's record, it is important to focus on the product. If the main product of the company is still lead, nuclear energy, asbestos, nasty pesticides, organochlorine chemicals or fossil fuels, it's greenwash.

Gain Your Sympathy by Adopting Environmental Lingo

Some polluting companies employ PR firms so talented at co-opting environment rhetoric you'd think they invented it. These corporations are some of the most powerful institutions in the world, so it is tempting to believe they are now environmentalists, since they really could help solve the problems facing the planet. For example, a manufacturer that uses toxic chemicals might call its process "pollution prevention," without telling you it has redesigned the phrase to include toxic waste incineration. After Rainforest Action Network (RAN) started its "Beyond Oil" campaign, BP countered with a motto of its own, saying BP stands for "Beyond Petroleum." But as we will see, BP means mainly that natural gas is "beyond petroleum," while RAN was referring to a renewable energy economy.

With green PR, it is important to study actions, not words and pictures. If Shell or BP tell us they are committed to solar power and the reduction of fossil fuel use, we have to look at how much they spend on new fossil fuel development to determine their sincerity. If fossil fuel investment dwarfs those in renewable energy, it's greenwash.

Avoid Regulations Claiming They Will Solve the Problem Themselves

A common form of greenwash is to claim deep personal and business interest in environmental solutions, while simultaneously lobbying to avoid regulations. A variant of this is the ad which rationalizes opposition to regulations by inventing or exaggerating economic costs. A corporate executive's personal fondness for nature and commitment to future generations is irrelevant if his main concern is shareholders and profit. If the company suggests endless delays and self-regulation as the solution, it's greenwash.

The examples of greenwash in the pages that follow are but a few examples of what has become almost an industry unto itself.

GREENWASH SNAPSHOT #1: BP

Recently BP, the world's second-largest oil company and one of the world's largest corporations, advertised its new identity as a leader in moving the world "Beyond Petroleum." Such leadership would benefit the world's climate and many of its communities immensely, according to British Petroleum. Sound too good to be true? Let's see.

BP says "Beyond Petroleum" means "being a global leader in producing the cleanest burning fossil fuel: Natural Gas." It's true that natural gas is not petroleum, but is it true that gas is a radical improvement over oil for our climate? In theory, natural gas emits somewhat less carbon dioxide than oil for the same energy produced, but when fugitive emissions, or leaks, are counted, the difference is slim to none. For the climate, natural gas is at best an incremental improvement over oil, and at worst a distraction from the challenge of moving our societies away from fossil fuels.[1]

That challenge is what is meant by "moving beyond petroleum," when used by environmental groups. Rainforest Action Network, for example, says their Beyond Oil campaign works to "move our societies out of our devastating dependence on fossil fuels and into renewable energy options. . . ."[2] BP's rebranding as the "Beyond Petroleum" company is perhaps the ultimate co-optation of environmentalists' language and message. Even apart from the twisting of language, BP's suggestion that producing more natural gas is somehow akin to global leadership is preposterous. Make that Beyond Preposterous.

BP Solar International promotional brochure. The copy proclaims, "Solar's time has come: this will be one of the great enterprises of the 21st century."

BP's claim to be "the largest producer of solar energy in the world" is a little more serious. Being number one for BP is so easy; it was achieved by spending $45 million to buy the Solarex solar energy corporation.[3] A week later, BP announced it would install solar panels in

200 gas stations around the world, claiming "we can fill you up by sunshine." But they are still filling you up WITH GASOLINE, the oil industry's lifeblood and a leading cause of global warming.

The cost of acquiring Solarex was a tiny fraction of the $26.8 billion it spent to buy ARCO, in order to increase BP's production capacity for oil.[4] BP has had plans to spend $5 billion over five years for oil exploration in Alaska alone. According to Greenpeace, BP spent more on their new eco-friendly logo last year than on renewable energy.[5] When a company spends more on advertising its environmental friendliness than on environmental actions, that's greenwash.

means being a global leader in producing the cleanest burning fossil fuel. Natural Gas.

beyond

means being the first company to introduce cleaner burning fuels to many of the world's most polluted cities.

means being the largest producer of solar energy in the world.

means starting a journey that will take the world's expectations of energy beyond what anyone can see today.

bp

beyond petroleum   www.bp.com

BP *"Beyond Petroleum"ad,* International Herald Tribune, *November 15, 2000. See box for copy.*

───────────── AD COPY ─────────────

BP "Beyond Petroleum"

Beyond...

means being a global leader in producing the cleanest burning fossil fuel. Natural Gas.

means being the first company to introduce cleaner burning fuels to many of the world's most polluted cities.

means being the largest producer of solar energy in the world.

means starting a journey that will take a world's expectations of energy beyond what anyone can see today.

BP's *Herald Tribune* ad is a bizarre classic of the greenwash genre. It is difficult to guess what their ad firm was trying to convey with the picture of partially submerged trees. Perhaps it's just an unusual nature photo, or perhaps it's meant to remind us of the frightening potential for rising sea levels and flooding from global warming. Or perhaps it's a Freudian slip, an unintentional reminder that BP's massive fossil-fuel production is responsible for a substantial portion of global carbon emissions and, therefore, climate change.

The ambiguity continues with the copy: "starting a journey that will take the world's expectations of energy beyond what anyone can see today"—pretentious stuff for a company serving mainly oil and gas, with just a sliver of solar on the side. Make that Beyond Pretentious.

BP has made at least one commitment that can be considered a serious one in controlling its power in society: a commitment to refrain from making political contributions anywhere in the world.[6] That commitment is unique among global companies. Nevertheless, on the environmental front, BP is still an oil company dedicated to growing its oil and gas business. That makes its fancy rhetoric mainly greenwash.

GREENWASH SNAPSHOT #2: COUNCIL FOR BIOTECHNOLOGY INFORMATION

Don't be fooled by the name: Council for Biotechnology Information is not an academic institution, nor is it about information. It's a consortium of the largest biotechnology companies, including Aventis, Dow Agro Sciences, DuPont and Monsanto. Its purpose is propaganda to win the public over to transgenic foods. Creating an objective-sounding group to front for special interests is part of the greenwash bag of tricks.

On April 1, 2000, the *New York Times* reported that "farmers are scaling back genetically altered crops."[7] Three days later, the Council was launched, with plans to spend up to $250 million on PR,[8] which exposed the public to bucolic farm scenes, clean natural environments, efficient-looking scientists and promises to cure diseases and end hunger. Biotechnology will help feed the world, says the industry.[9] Those who oppose genetic engineering are selfish, liberal, wealthy western consumers without concern for the Third World poor. This is greenwash with a guilt trip.

From a promotional report cover for the Council for Biotechnology Information. The copy reads, in part, "realizing the promise of innovation yesterday, today and tomorrow" and "good ideas are growing." Ironically, given its name, the council lobbies hard against labeling genetically engineered food—that is, actually providing "biotechnology information" to consumers.

The Council's PR offensive comes after a public relations fiasco led by Monsanto. Secrecy and contempt for consumers, through opposition to labeling, have been parts of the modus operandi of the big biotech firms as they have introduced transgenic crops over the last five years. This secrecy backfired badly in Europe,[10] where the public was extremely suspicious of genetically engineered foods. Thus, the belated attempt at transparency.

The biotech industry has succeeded in gaining a de facto approval at high levels of the U.N. The inclusion of Aventis and Novartis in the Global Compact implies that their basic products have been accepted globally, when, in fact, the debate over them is still quite intense. As already noted in Chapter Three, the UNDP has essentially sided with the industry in giving transgenic foods a positive plug in its Human Development Report, though many of its NGO partners intensely resent this technology.

The money spent on advertising the benefits of genetic engineering is an investment not only in public acceptance, but also in avoiding regulations, such as labeling, that the industry dislikes. This form of greenwash—image making to avoid regulation—is one of the most common.

GREENWASH SNAPSHOT #3: CHEVRON

Begun in 1985, Chevron's "People Do" series has pioneered the art of corporate greenwash. The ad campaign, which ran for more than fifteen years, is a textbook case of successful greenwashing. It began when Chevron asked itself whether or not it would pay to tailor an advertising campaign to a "hostile audience" of "societally conscious" people concerned about such issues as offshore oil drilling.[11]

Produced at a cost of $5 to $10 million a year, the campaign consisted of an expanding series of advertisements, each of which featured a different Chevron People Do project. The ads have publicized a butterfly "preserve" at the El Segundo refinery, artificial reefs made of old gas station storage tanks the company sunk off the coast of Florida, efforts to protect grizzly bears near one of its drilling sites in Montana and artificial kit fox dens in California's Central Valley. Other advertisements publicize company projects in Australia and Canada.

Chevron has spent much more on promoting its image through these projects than it did on the projects themselves: producing one thirty-second advertisement costs $200,000, while the El Segundo butterfly program costs only $5,000 a year.[12] This does not include the millions Chevron spends buying magazine space and TV airtime.

The Desert
That Glistened
With Water.

Southeastern New Mexico is
home to mesquite and chaparral,
mesas and horizons that shimmer
with heat. For animals
of this parched land,
survival comes with
water. So people who work
nearby helped design and build
a system of dozens of unique
watering units that gather, store
and distribute water to bobcats,
antelopes, hawks and more.
Quenching nature's thirst and
giving it a chance to survive.

Chevron

People Do.

www.peopledo.com

©1999 Chevron Corporation

One ad in Chevron's landmark "People Do" campaign. This ran in Harper's *magazine in October 1999. See box for ad copy.*

AD COPY

Chevron "People Do"

The Desert That Glistened With Water.

Southeastern New Mexico is home to mesquite and
chaparral, mesas and horizons that shimmer with heat.
For animals of this parched land, survival comes with
water. So people who work nearby helped design and
build a system of dozens of unique watering units that
gather, store and distribute water to bobcats, antelopes,
hawks and more. Quenching nature's thirst and giving it
a chance to survive.

People Do.

—*Harper's*, October 1999

The ads are misleading. A number of the People Do projects, such
as programs to protect the grizzly bear in Montana, waterfowl in
Mississippi, eagles in Wyoming and the kit fox in California, are programs that are mandatory under the law.[13] Yet the advertisements
either fail to mention or downplay this fact. Herbert Chao Gunther,
Director of the Public Media Center in San Francisco, comments that
"the ads are a selective presentation of the facts with a lack of context.
Chevron implies that maybe we don't need a regulatory framework
because the oil companies are taking care of it."[14]

It does appear that one major factor motivating Chevron's People
Do campaign is the transnational company's deregulatory agenda. An
investigation of People Do by a local San Francisco television station
discovered that although Chevron sells gasoline across much of the
country, the corporation has only aired its ads in the top three oil producing states of the continental U.S., California, Texas and Louisiana,
locations where it drills for and refines most of its oil and, conse-
quently, where it is most heavily regulated.[15] Confronted with this
evidence, Chevron spokespeople insist that People Do is not a "political advocacy program" (if it were found to be so, their advertising
might no longer be tax deductible). But the only other place in the
U.S. where Chevron airs its People Do advertisements is in
Washington, D.C., hardly a nationally significant gasoline market.[16]

Despite public skepticism and environmentalist criticism, the
People Do strategy seems to have worked. Polls Chevron conducted

in California two years after the campaign began show it had become the oil corporation people trusted most to protect the environment. The greenwash also paid off at the gas pump: among those who saw the commercials, Chevron sales increased by 10 percent, while among a target audience of the potentially antagonistic socially concerned types, sales jumped by 22 percent. Thus, Chevron's person in charge of public affairs research could conclude that "it does pay to advertise to hostile audiences."[17]

If the goal were sustainability, Chevron would be investing more in alternative energy sources and conservation than in purchasing green PR and other oil companies (the corporation is now called ChevronTexaco).

GREENWASH SNAPSHOT #4: FORD

Ford placed a striking advertisement in the May 1996 issue of *Popular Science*—a lovely mirage-like image of a silver car in a field of beautiful pink and red flowers. Puffy white clouds and majestic purple mountains form a dreamy backdrop for Ford's new car. An hour or so of TV watching in the U.S. reveals that Ford is not the only company that links beautiful natural imagery to cars, but it remains one of the more absurd juxtapositions and a cornerstone of greenwash.

In the ad, Ford unabashedly links itself to three environmentally devastating industrial sectors—automobiles, aluminum and plastics— and still manages to put an earth-friendly face on its product. In a string of short, choppy phrases, Ford suggests that its highly recyclable, fuel-efficient, aluminum-bodied car maintains all the safety of previous, heavier cars made of steel. What Ford neglects to state, however, is how much of the "recyclable" material will or can actually be recycled. Just saying that something is recyclable does not mean that it is made from recycled material or that it will be recycled at some point in its life.

Ford adroitly focuses the prospective customer's attention on subtle design changes and away from the larger problem of the car itself. Motor vehicle transport is responsible for about one-fifth of all U.S. CO_2 emissions.[18] Fuel emissions are only one of the many environmentally destructive aspects of the automobile society. In the United States alone, almost half of all urban space is set aside for automobile use, while some 10 percent of the arable land has been paved over.[19] Quality of life in cities around the world is declining because of

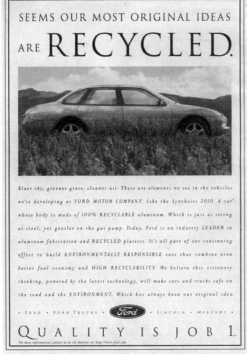

Ford "Recycled" ad, which ran in Popular Science *in May 1996. See box for ad copy.*

AD COPY

Ford

Seems our most original ideas are recycled.

Bluer sky, greener grass, cleaner air. These are elements we see in the vehicles we're developing at FORD MOTOR COMPANY. Like the Synthesis 2010. A car whose body is made of 100% RECYCLABLE aluminum. Which is just as strong as steel, yet gentler on the gas pump. Today, Ford is an industry LEADER in aluminum fabrication and RECYCLED plastics. It's all part of our continuing effort to build ENVIRONMENTALLY RESPONSIBLE cars that combine even better fuel economy and HIGH RECYCLABILITY. We believe this visionary thinking, powered by the latest technology, will make cars and trucks safe on the road and on the ENVIRONMENT. Which has always been our original idea.

—*Popular Science,* May 1999

traffic congestion and pollution, and each year nearly a half million people die from traffic accidents.[20]

Ford claims that the Synthesis 2010 is a part of the company's effort to build "ENVIRONMENTALLY RESPONSIBLE cars. . . ." In the years since 1996, Ford, like other major automakers, has continued to build more SUVs. Looking back, we can see the ad clearly for what it was: greenwash.

On April 15, 2000, the Ford Motor Company sponsored the Heroes for the Planet concert in San Francisco. The concert and media extravaganza was the kickoff for one of the most expensive environmental advertising campaigns ever. At the time, Ford announced that all corporate brand advertising would have an environmental theme. It expected to spend as much on green advertising as it does to roll out a new line of cars.[21]

For this advertising campaign, Ford brought in the services of one of the best antienvironmental PR firms in the business, Hill and Knowlton. John Stauber of *PR Watch* says, "Hill and Knowlton are the propagandists for the worst polluting corporations on the planet."[22]

On Earth Day 2000, Ford sponsored the Heroes for the Planet concert in San Francisco, kicking off one of the most expensive advertising campaigns ever. Photograph by Joshua Karliner.

Ford also bought nearly 40 percent of *Time Magazine's* special Earth Day 2000 edition.[23] Ford was the exclusive advertiser in two special issues for *Time for Kids*, reaching 2.8 million students in elementary schools in the U.S. alone.

Meanwhile, according to the March 2000 report "Pollution Lineup" by the Union of Concerned Scientists:

- Ford's cars are the worst carbon emitters of any major automaker.
- Ford's light trucks are the worst carbon emitters of any major automaker.
- Ford is the second-worst polluter overall of any automaker.
- Ford's fuel efficiency trend is the worst of any automaker.
- In the ten years after global warming first became a public concern, average vehicle emissions for Ford increased by 7.4 percent.
- Between 1990 and 1998, emissions from new Ford cars rose from about 21 million tons of CO_2 to about 27 million tons, just a hair below General Motors, the larger company.[24]

Ford's environmentally themed advertising and promotions have been going on for at least six years, both before and after environmentalist William Clay Ford took over the company. In that time, they have continued to lobby against better fuel efficiency, and they have fallen behind Japanese automakers in producing cleaner cars.[25]

It could lead one to believe the PR is just greenwash.

GREENWASH SNAPSHOT #5: MITSUBISHI

No animal is more symbolic of the environmental movement than the whale. So when Mitsubishi claimed to be operating "in harmony" with the gray whale in Mexico as a way of promoting a planned salt-evaporation facility in a calving ground for the species, it earned them a place in the annals of greenwash.

In this case, the greenwash was unsuccessful; the mammoth salt-evaporation plant Mitsubishi, together with the Mexican government, planned to build in the middle of a California gray whale calving ground was never begun. However, the reality of Mitsubishi's plans was quite different from the rhetoric. In fact, this industrial salt facility, which was to be the largest in the world, threatened the gray whale, along with several other species of wildlife.[26] Its site, Laguna

San Ignacio, is located in the middle of a United Nations' Biosphere
Reserve in Baja California, a zone where any kind of development is
officially "restricted" and to which gray whales migrate each year.[27]
Moreover, the image of benign table salt as the product of the plant
was misleading. One of the main uses of the salt was to be as feed-
stock for chlorine production, which in turn is the basis for many of
industrial society's most toxic chemicals, such as DDT and other
chlorinated pesticides, PCBs, perchloroethylene, trichloroethylene,
CFCs and more.[28]

Greenwash exhibit "A" is a slick full-page advertisement that
Mitsubishi Corporation placed in *The New York Times* in June 1995.
The ad was in response to harsh criticism from environmentalists, and
it claimed that Mitsubishi had been operating "in harmony with the
whales for more than two decades."

Greenwash exhibit "A": Mitsubishi's New York Times *ad, which appeared June 27,
1995. See box for ad copy.*

—————— **AD COPY** ——————

Greenwash exhibit "A": Mitsubishi

When Your Neighbors Are This Precious, You Learn to Take Care.

Every winter, the gray whale migrates south to mate and calve.

Some of these great mammals stop in quiet lagoons in Baja, California. We know because Mitsubishi Corporation, working with the Mexican government, has supported a salt production facility in the region, in harmony with the whales, for more than two decades.

The joint venture company, Exportadora de Sal S.A. de C.V. (ESSA), is proud of the existing Baja solar evaporation salt collection facility at Guerrero Negro. Mitsubishi Corporation is pleased to support this effort to harvest a valuable renewable resource. Recently, ESSA has begun to explore the development of new salt production in the region near San Ignacio lagoon that will result in improved economic conditions and a better future for local families.

But first, we must ensure that the gray whale and other wildlife populations will not be harmed. In accordance with guidelines from the Mexican environmental authorities on this project, ESSA will commission a further environmental impact assessment of the proposed new facility, which will be reviewed by a group of internationally recognized scientists and members of the academic community. This new facility must be compatible with the local Vizcaino Desert Biosphere Reserve, the gray whale, and other natural assets. Mitsubishi Corporation takes its responsibilities for environmental stewardship very seriously. Until we are sure that nature and mankind can live in harmony, we will not go forward.

"We believe a business cannot continue to exist without the trust and respect of society for its environmental performance."

—Mitsubishi Corporation

—— *Ad copy continued on next page.* ——

AD COPY, continued.

Statement of Environmental Principles

Sustainable environmental stewardship has to integrate environmental, economic, and a broad range of social considerations. Mitsubishi Corporation has demonstrated a long-standing commitment to conservation and the wise use of all natural resources. This philosophy of stewardship governs our trade and investment activities worldwide and leads us to the following commitments regarding the San Ignacio project.

- Mitsubishi Corporation, along with our Mexican government partners, will proceed only when scientifically documented and approved plans to protect the environment are in place.

- We support an independent assessment to assure protection of the local environment, gray whales, and other wildlife.

- We will proceed only if the project is environmentally sound and can be so sustained over the long term.

—*New York Times,* June 27, 1995

Greenwash exhibit "B" is a container of table salt from Mitsubishi's joint venture company, ESSA; emblazoned on the front is the image of a gray whale "spyhopping," while on the back the consumer information provided is that the salt is "produced . . . through a natural process that is completely compatible with the environment."

Fortunately, environmentalists in Mexico and the United States, as well as the local fisher-folk communities in Laguna San Ignacio, saw through the greenwash. By bringing pressure on the government and the company through a multiyear international campaign, they succeeded in canceling this destructive project, in spite of Mitsubishi's public relations machine.[29]

Mitsubishi Greenwash exhibit "B": Mexican table salt manufactured by Mitsubishi's joint venture company, ESSA. On the back, the label reads "High quality salt produced with brine obtained through the natural process of solar evaporation of sea water, which is completely compatible with the environment." Photograph by Joshua Karliner.

GREENWASH SNAPSHOT #6: MONSANTO

"Sustainable development will be a primary emphasis in everything we do," said former Monsanto CEO Robert Shapiro.[30] Monsanto would have us believe it is a leader of sustainable development.

Monsanto is unquestionably a world leader in agricultural genetic engineering and has staked its future on that business. The company has also run a slick campaign to convince a skeptical public that its genetic manipulation is a key to "sustainable development."

Monsanto tugs at our heartstrings by pointing to the gap between a growing world population and a diminishing food supply. As CEO Robert Shapiro wrote in the introduction to Monsanto's 1996 *Environmental Review*, the use of genetically engineered crops "will help immensely in closing the gap between hungry people and adequate food supplies."[31] But will genetically engineered crops actually help feed the hungry? The evidence says no.

Monsanto's recombinant Bovine Growth Hormone (rBGH), for example, is designed to increase milk production, but the U.S. already has an oversupply of milk,[32] so increased production drives down the price that farmers receive. In addition, rBGH is so costly that dairy farmers in the Third World will be unable to purchase it,[33] excluding them from any of the "benefits" of this technology.

The company's Roundup Ready soybeans are not designed to increase yield, though their ease of use might allow farmers to plant more soybeans while increasing use of the Roundup herbicide in those marginal acres. However, most soybeans end up in oil or become minor ingredients in a wide variety of processed foods never seen by undernourished peasants in Bangladesh or Chad.

Yieldgard corn mostly goes to animal feed. None of Monsanto's transgenic canola, sugar beets, cotton, corn or potatoes is designed to put food in the mouths of hungry children.[34]

population

THE RACE IS ON.

food supply

Part of an ad from Monsanto's "Food • Health • Hope" campaign; this ran in the New York Times *in December 1998. See box for ad copy.*

The myth that world hunger is a result of global food shortages was debunked years ago. More germane issues for the poor include access to the food that exists and access to land to grow their own. High technology and high-input cash crops are not the answer to this problem. They are, however, helpful to Monsanto's appetite for increased control over food production.

CEO Shapiro wrote, "There have been times in Monsanto's ninety-four-year history when we, like others, weren't as aware of our actions as we should have been. These days have been over for a long time."[35]

Have they really?

AD COPY

Monsanto
The Race is On.

Population grows by about 230,000 people every day. At this rate, the world will need twice as much food in just 50 years. Extra farmland to grow this simply doesn't exist. At Monsanto, we are working with a promising tool in the effort to provide more food—biotechnology. It's biotechnology that has allowed farmers to dramatically increase crop yields without more farmland. While growing them in a way that's more sustainable— with less pesticide, less fossil fuel, and less impact on the environment. It's many case, it even allows them to grow crops that are more nutritious. Biotechnology. It's one way food supply can continue to grow. While, at the same time, becoming more sustainable and more nutritious for a growing population.

Monsanto
Food • Health • Hope™

—*New York Times*, December 8, 1998

GREENWASH SNAPSHOT #7: THE NUCLEAR ENERGY INSTITUTE

The Nuclear Energy Institute (NEI) is a greenwash veteran. In 1991, the organization, then known as the U.S. Council for Energy Awareness, ran an ad saying, "Trees aren't the only plants that are good for the atmosphere." That ad pictures a lovely lake, trees and blue skies, co-existing harmoniously with the characteristic dome of a nuke.[36]

In 1999, Public Citizen and Nuclear Information Research Service filed a petition to the Federal Trade Commission (FTC) alleging that NEI environmental ads with similar claims were false and misleading. The FTC agreed that the ads were inaccurate, but also ruled that it was political, not commercial, speech and therefore protected.[37]

In another ad, they have chosen an adolescent girl to represent the renewed aspirations of the nuclear energy industry. The choice is especially ironic, because children are more susceptible to the effects of radiation than adults, since their cells are still dividing. Furthermore, women of childbearing age or girls still developing reproductive capability bear a second burden: the danger to their future offspring.

An ad for the Nuclear Energy Institute that ran in the New Yorker *in April, 2001. See box for ad copy.*

The industry complements these ads with a strong dose of old-fashioned lobbying: their message has found a friendly reception in the Bush Administration. A few days after his staff met with nuclear industry officials, Vice President Dick Cheney said, "If you want to do something about carbon dioxide emissions then you ought to build nuclear power plants."[38] Since Dick Cheney has never been very concerned about carbon emissions, this statement is as opportunistic as the nuclear industry's stance on "clean air."

The reality is that energy efficiency and renewables, such as solar and wind, are cheaper than nukes. Each cent spent on a nuclear kilowatt could have bought two kilowatts worth of efficiency. Because of that kind of lost opportunity costs, according to the Rocky Mountain Institute, buying nuclear power will actually make climate change worse than if the cheapest renewable options were bought instead.[39] In addition, when you include CO_2 generated in the production of nuclear fuel, during mining of uranium for example, nukes emit about four times as much as renewable energy sources.[40]

The tag line, "Clean air is <u>so</u> 21st Century" makes nuclear power seem like the technology of the future. What kind of industry would continue to generate waste that remains dangerously radioactive for a hundred thousand years? A twentieth-century industry, of course.

GREENWASH SNAPSHOT #8: PHILIP MORRIS

According to the World Health Organization (WHO), Philip Morris, along with British American Tobacco and other tobacco companies, worked for years to undermine WHO tobacco control initiatives.[41] These corporations' own documents show that they viewed WHO as one of their main enemies and that they attempted to influence WHO and other U.N. agencies, along with representatives of developing countries, to resist tobacco control efforts. The WHO report states that "the tobacco companies' activities slowed and undermined effective tobacco control programs around the world."[42]

Yet Philip Morris, the largest U.S.-based tobacco corporation, presents itself as a humanitarian company. Its television ad series, "Working to make a difference," tells us moving stories of real people's struggles and gives a not-so-subtle implication that Philip Morris has been the one to help these people out of a jam through corporate charity.

Tobacco products kill about 4 million people annually worldwide and that figure may rise to some 10 million, according to the World Health Organization.[43] Philip Morris is the world's largest cigarette manufacturer, with just about half of the U.S. market, and 14 percent of the market in the rest of the world.[44] Philip Morris products are responsible for an astounding number of premature and preventable deaths for a single corporation. Many observers believe that Philip Morris executives have consciously made their products more addictive and lied about it. Flouting science, they also denied the connection between smoking and cancer and the many other tobacco-related health problems, until they could not longer refute the facts. They have spent millions to evade liability in court for the consequences of their corporate behavior. So far, despite growing legal and regulatory constraints, and despite widespread animosity towards the company, it remains enormously profitable.

Nevertheless, at some point Philip Morris realized that things could go terribly wrong, as things had for asbestos companies driven into bankruptcy by lawsuits. It chose a two-pronged strategy to protect its financial future: First it diversified, mainly by buying Kraft, the largest food company in the U.S., and, more recently, Nabisco; second, it launched a giant corporate image campaign with some interesting features. The company had taken an enormous risk by advertising the fact that Kraft was a Philip Morris company. Some of the ads discuss Kraft's charitable works, but always mention that Kraft is "part of the Philip Morris family of companies." Their calculation is that Kraft's benign reputation would rub off on Philip Morris, rather than PM's horrific reputation tainting Kraft brands. They may end up wishing the American public had continued to believe Kraft was independent. Infact, a Massachusetts-based nonprofit group, has organized a boycott of Kraft foods as a strategy to put pressure on Philip Morris, and the group believes that the boycott will grow as people learn of Kraft's connection to Marlboro and Virginia Slims.[45]

Unlike typical greenwash, there is no connection made between the company's products and their good works. No one smokes, no brand names are mentioned and there isn't even a hint of Philip Morris's main business. It's as if they recognize that the dissonance in mentioning Marlboro and philanthropy in the same breath would be too harsh. Yet at the same time, it allows them to get the Philip Morris name back on TV, even though cigarette ads are banned. Pretty clever.

What about the "good works" of Philip Morris? Is there anything wrong with giving money to Meals-On-Wheels, battered women's shelters and flood relief? Of course not. When you run a shelter, a concert series or a conservation trust, and government money has dried up—largely because of policies that favor the same rich individuals and corporations you are now dependent on for private donations, but that's a longer story—you are likely to accept money from just about anywhere.

Nevertheless, the ads are misleading. While the actress in the ad about the battered wife makes many good points about the dynamics of domestic violence, it all goes awry when implying that Philip Morris is a friend of women. Ever since "You've Come a Long Way Baby," the perverse association of cigarettes and woman's emancipation has led large numbers of women to join the ranks of smokers. In fact, six years after Virginia Slims went on the market, the rate of smoking among twelve-year-old girls jumped a startling 110 percent. By 1997, 35 percent of female high school students were smokers, up from 27 percent six years earlier, according to the Centers for Disease Control.[46]

The ad also makes it seem like Philip Morris is especially concerned about children. However, as Infact has documented in their "Making A Killing" video,[47] the Marlboro Man is specifically designed to attract young smokers, and, especially in Asia, Philip Morris continues its tradition of luring young people into a lifelong, lethal habit.

A look at the numbers shows that Philip Morris largesse is not only self-serving, but also stingy: They say they spent $115 million in 1999 on charities, making them the third-largest corporate giver in the country.[48] They are also the ninth-largest company by sales ($61.8 bil-

A storyboard for a Philip Morris–produced television ad. See box for ad copy.

lion), and the eighth-most profitable U.S. company ($7.7 billion), so their place in the top-ten charitable givers makes them only slightly more generous than their peers. One hundred fifteen million dollars is approximately 1.5 percent of Philip Morris's domestic profits.[49] That's slightly higher than average for an U.S. corporation, but not wildly generous. Given the damage they have done, their giving does not begin to balance the scales.

AD COPY

Philip Morris TV Ad: "Laura"

Laura voiceover: When I was nine months pregnant . . . my husband beat me. . . . One night, he came after me with a knife and barely missed our son. I left. My kids and I ended up at a shelter. I realized, it wasn't my fault. Women are beaten every day. And if we'd stayed, I knew he would hurt my daughter.

Announcer voiceover: All across the country battered women and children are starting new lives . . . thanks in part to Philip Morris, one of the largest supporters of programs . . . that feed, shelter and counsel victims of domestic violence.

Laura voiceover: But what frightened me most was that if we'd stayed . . . I was putting my son at risk of becoming a batterer himself. I grew up in a very loving home. My kids deserve to grow up in one too.

Announcer voiceover: Working to make a difference. The people of Philip Morris. (Kraft, Miller, and Philip Morris USA logos)

In 2000, Philip Morris spent $94 million to advertise Marlboro, $118 million to advertise Kraft brands, $92 million promoting Miller beer and $142 million on corporate image advertising.[50] When a company spends more to boast about humanitarian programs than on the programs themselves, that's greenwash.

GREENWASH SNAPSHOT #9: SOUTHERN COMPANY

Southern Company is the second largest electricity producer in the United States. It also operates, or plans to operate, in China, the Philippines, India, Pakistan, Bangladesh, Argentina, the Bahamas,

Brazil, Chile, Germany, and Trinidad and Tobago. Its environmental initiatives, for better or worse, are almost as widespread. However, it seems that for each environmental initiative that could protect the climate, Southern provides it own destructive countermeasure.

We will continue to improve

the environment in

our communities and

protect public health

while supplying reliable,

affordable energy to

the people we serve.

Partial cover of Southern Company's "Environmental Progress Report 2001: Our Environmental Commitment." Taglines include "Southern Company. Energy to Serve Your World®."

For example, Southern signed up for the Clinton administration's Climate Challenge Participation Accord and was praised by former Energy Secretary Bill Richardson for its electric car program for employees.[51] Yet at the same time, Southern was an active member of the Global Climate Coalition (GCC), a group of powerful corporations aiming to derail the Kyoto Protocol negotiations. Southern was even a member of the committee that created the GCC's advertising campaign to demonize the Kyoto Protocol and developing countries in the eyes of the American public. They later abandoned the GCC.

One of Southern's better-publicized environmental initiatives was the electric cars it donated to the National Zoo in Washington, D.C. Electric cars could help reduce greenhouse gas emissions by reducing gasoline use, but if the plants they are plugging into are fired by coal, the emissions reduced at the tailpipe will be offset by those of the power plant.

The main point to keep in mind about Southern is that most of its electricity, 73 percent, is generated by the burning of coal, the most carbon-intensive fossil fuel and the worst fuel for the climate. Nationwide, Southern is the second-largest direct emitter of CO_2 at just under 150 million tons per year.[52] This is comparable to the emissions from all of Texaco's oil and gas or with the emissions from all of Argentina. Southern has also been the country's second-largest emitter of acid-rain-causing sulfur dioxide and third-largest emitter of the air pollutant nitrogen oxide, according to the Natural Resources Defense Council.[53]

The electric cars, the tree planting, the partnerships, the "clean coal" programs and the "Green Lights" and "Earth Comfort" programs can't turn coal green. Southern's record remains primarily that of a major coal-burning company, with all the air pollution and greenhouse gas emissions that entails.

GREENWASH SNAPSHOT #10: ROYAL DUTCH SHELL

During the Sixth U.N. Conference on Climate Change at The Hague, Shell, the world's third-largest oil company, continued its clever but misleading series, "Profits or Principles," with the ad pictured here.

The ad is pretty, of course, and it sounds reasonable, caring and honest.

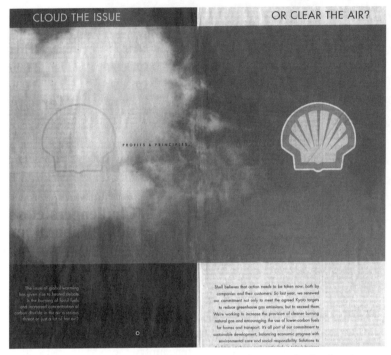

Shell ad, which ran in the Financial Times *in November 2000. See box for ad copy.*

Shell asks: "Is the burning of fossil fuels and increased concentration of carbon dioxide in the air a serious threat or just a lot of hot air?" It sounds like a tough question, but it's not. There is overwhelming scientific opinion that both fossil fuel use and CO_2 emissions are serious threats. The main reason for the "hot air" theory is a major effort by the oil industry, among others, to discredit climate change science in the eyes of policy makers and the public.

Shell says, "Last year, we renewed our commitment not only to meet the agreed Kyoto targets to reduce greenhouse gas emissions, but to exceed them." This is a fine step, but not nearly as significant as it might seem. Like the other fossil fuel giants, Shell's impact on the climate stems not primarily from its use of oil and gas, but from its production. Oil produced by Shell alone accounts for more carbon dioxide than most countries in the world.[54] Steps to address this much larger role would be significant, but instead, Shell continues its worldwide effort to locate and produce more oil and gas.

Meanwhile, other ads in the "Profits or Principles" series tout Shell's commitment to renewable energy sources, featuring Shell photos of lush green forests accompanied by earnest discussion of this purported commitment. However, according to Greenpeace, Shell spends a miniscule 0.6 percent of its annual investments on renewables.[55] In true greenwash fashion, Shell's actions do not match its words.

Says Shell, "It's all part of our commitment to sustainable development." Their ad writer should read an essay in Shell's own glossy booklet "Profits and Principles—Does There Have to Be a Choice?" Buried in the expensive and lovely pages of that publication is this nugget of truth: "A sustainable oil company is a contradiction in terms."

AD COPY

Shell

Cloud the Issue or Clear the Air?

The issue of global warming has given rise to heated debate. Is the burning of fossil fuels and increased concentration of carbon dioxide in the air a serious threat or just a lot of hot air?

Shell believes that action needs to be taken now, both by companies and their customers. So last year, we renewed our commitment not only to meet the agreed Kyoto targets to reduce greenhouse gas emissions, but to exceed them. We're working to increase the provision of cleaner burning natural gas and encouraging the use of lower-carbon fuels for homes and transport. It's all part of our commitment to sustainable development, balancing economic progress with environmental care and social responsibility. Solutions to the future won't come easily, particularly in today's business climate, but you can't find them if you don't keep looking.

We welcome your input. Contact us on the internet at www.shell.com. Email us at tell-shell@si.shell.com or write to us at: "The Profits & Principles Debate," Shell International Ltd, Shell Centre London SE1 7NA UK.

—*Financial Times*, November 14, 2000

CHAPTER SEVEN

Bluewash Snapshots

Many corporations are major culprits in human rights violations and contributors to inequality around the world, so it is perhaps natural that they are pioneers of a new shade of greenwash, advertising and rhetoric not around ecological protection but around anti-poverty programs, development and human rights. We call this "bluewash," blue being the color of the U.N. flag and helmet and also standing for the blue collars of workers fighting for their rights. By extension, "bluewash" refers to advertising with a humanitarian or human rights theme. Oil is one industry involved in this deception; tobacco is another.

A classic bluewash method is for a company to join the U.N. Global Compact (see Chapter Three and Appendix A), then act in ways that violate the letter or spirit of the Compact's principles. Based on research by our colleagues in the Alliance for a Corporate-Free U.N., we can report that several companies have already behaved in a manner that violates the spirit of the Global Compact principles they signed. The following are snapshots or synopses of detailed articles prepared by members of the Alliance and published on the CorpWatch website as part of our effort to document the inherent contradictions of the Global Compact. These articles do not represent a complete inventory of Global Compact violations, but rather a small sampling of what we might find in a comprehensive investigation. (The full articles are available on our website at www.corpwatch.org/un.) The companies profiled in this chapter either appeared on the initial list of companies at the Global Compact launch event or in the list of participating companies on the Global Compact website as of May 24, 2002.[1]

Bluewash Snapshot #1: Aventis

Since Aventis signed on to the Global Compact in July 2000, its genetically engineered StarLink™ corn has illegally contaminated the food supply and seed stock in the U.S. The contamination of other corn varieties significantly impacts links throughout the food chain, from farmers, grain elevators and food processors, to retail grocers and consumers. Without a system of segregation or the ability to control pollen drift, StarLink contaminated much of the U.S. corn supply. The full costs of this contamination continue to emerge; however, current estimates run in the hundreds of billions of dollars.

A look at the company's behavior regarding StarLink shows that before and after signing the Compact, Aventis violated Global Compact's Principle Seven, which is drawn from the Rio Declaration and supports "a precautionary approach to environmental challenges."[2]

Bluewash Snapshot #2: Nike

Since 1997, Nike has continually failed to uphold "freedom of association and the effective recognition of the right to collective bargaining," which is Principle Three of the Global Compact. Nike made a commitment to respect this right in 1997 when, along with other giant shoe and garment manufacturers like Reebok, Adidas, Liz Claiborne and Patagonia, it signed the Fair Labor Association's voluntary workplace code of conduct. Violations of Principle Three and related accounts of repression, firings, violence and threats are found in Nike production factories in China, Indonesia, Thailand, Cambodia and Mexico. In addition, Nike has been actively involved in lobbying Washington, D.C., against using trade policy to pressure China to respect workers' rights.[3]

Bluewash Snapshot #3: Rio Tinto

In 2000, the Indonesian government's National Human Rights Commission investigated allegations of abuses at the Rio Tinto's Kelian gold mine and found egregious violations. Since the mine opened in 1992, the Commission revealed, the Indonesian military and company security forcibly evicted traditional miners, burned down villages and arrested and detained protestors. Local people have systematically lost homes, lands, gardens, fruit trees, forest resources, family graves and the right to mine for gold in the river, according to the Human Rights Commission. Kelian employees have also been named in a number of incidents of sexual harassment, rape and violence against local women between 1987 and 1997, including abuse and rape committed by senior company staff against local Dayak women.

Rio Tinto, which has headquarters in the U.K. and Australia, also is accused of environmental abuses affecting the health of the surrounding community. The Kelian mine produces over fourteen tons of gold per year using the cyanide heap-leaching process, which produces contaminated tailings. The tailings are held in a dam and treated in a polishing pond near the Kelian River. Water from the polishing pond pours into the river through an outlet. The company claims that the water is clean; meanwhile, the community says that people cannot drink or bathe in the water because it causes skin lesions and stomach aches.

Two articles on the CorpWatch website (www.corpwatch.org) document Rio Tinto's violation of Principle One of the Global Compact, which requests companies to "support and respect the protection of international human rights within their sphere of influence," and Principle Eight, which asks business to "undertake initiatives to promote greater environmental responsibility." [4]

Bluewash Snapshot #4: International Chamber of Commerce

The ICC, a lobby group with over 7,000 corporate members, is a prominent partner in U.N. Secretary General Kofi Annan's Global Compact and has played a key role in shaping it from the start. While the ICC has provided momentum to the Global Compact, it also seriously undermines its credibility.

The ICC has a long history of vigorous lobbying to weaken international environmental treaties, and these efforts have continued even after the group has pledged support for the Global Compact principles. Examples of such treaties include the Kyoto Protocol, the Convention on Biodiversity and the Basel Convention against trade in toxic waste. In all these U.N. negotiations, the International Chamber's obstructive lobbying runs counter to the Global Compact principles to which it allegedly subscribes. Rather than "supporting a precautionary approach to environmental challenges" (Principle Seven) and rather than undertaking "initiatives to promote greater environmental responsibility" (Principle Eight), the ICC promotes a narrow commercial agenda, dominated by some of the world's most environmentally irresponsible corporations. [5]

Bluewash Snapshot #5: Unilever

In March 2001, residents of Kodaikanal, a pretty hill retreat in Southern India, caught the Anglo-Dutch multinational Unilever red-handed when they uncovered a dumpsite with toxic mercury-laced waste from a thermometer factory run by Unilever's Indian subsidiary, Hindustan Lever. The 7.4-ton stockpile of crushed mercury-laden glass was found in torn sacks, spilling onto the ground in a busy scrapyard located near a school. Company officials denied and downplayed the dumpsite, eventually refusing even to engage researchers in dialogue about the issue.

At Kodaikanal, Unilever's behavior violates the environmental principles of the Global Compact that require signatories to "support a precautionary approach to environmental challenges" (Principle Seven), "undertake initiatives to promote greater environmental responsibility" (Principle Eight) and promote the "diffusion of environmentally friendly technologies" (Principle Nine). Allegations that the company has employed a double standard in relation to worker safety indicate a violation of Principle Six, "the elimination of discrimination in respect of employment and occupation."[6]

Bluewash Snapshot #6: Norsk Hydro

Late in 2000, Norsk Hydro, a Norwegian corporation with investments in light metals, oil, petrochemicals and agriculture, faced a crisis in the Eastern Indian state of Orissa, where it is a partner in a $1 billion bauxite/alumina project. On December 16, 2000, three tribal men—two aged twenty-five and one aged forty-five—were shot dead near their village. Nine others were seriously injured. The three who died were among several hundred local residents fleeing armed police, who had been called in to quell protests against the project.

Norsk Hydro and its partners did decide to "temporarily curtail" the project "pending a lower level of tension," but that response does not reveal the company's role in fueling tensions leading to the protestors' deaths. Allowing tensions to reach a point where the police violently repress dissent reflects a violation of Principle Two, to "make sure their own corporations are not complicit in human rights abuses." The failure to abandon the project in keeping with the wishes of the local people is a violation of Principle One, to "support and respect the protection of international human rights within their sphere of influence."[7]

Bluewash Snapshot #7: Bayer

Bayer AG, based in Leverkusen, Germany, is one of the world's largest chemical and biotechnology firms, with a long history of unethical behavior, including close relations with the Third Reich (as part of the chemical conglomerate I. G. Farben), involvement in a "School for

Chemical Warfare" and selling of HIV-tainted blood-clotting products. More recently, Bayer was one of the companies that took South African government to court for allowing the production of generic versions of HIV drugs.[8]

Bayer's record on health and environmental issues is extremely controversial. The use of hazardous pesticides, excessive antibiotics, HIV drug pricing, and most recently, its response to the anthrax scare in the U.S., are just some areas where Bayer's behavior has been highly questionable. In addition, Bayer's reach is global, with their policies and products affecting people from Brazil, to South Africa, to Europe.[9]

Bayer's involvement as a "founding member"[10] of the Global Compact fits too conveniently with their parallel record as a member of lobby groups that consistently work to undermine U.N. agreements and principles. Among these are the ICC, the Transatlantic Business Dialogue, the European Round Table of Industrialists, the Global Crop Protection Federation and EuropaBio, Europe's leading biotech lobby group.[11]

Bayer attended the launch of the Global Compact in July 2000 and is listed by the UN as a Global Compact company.[12] Yet, at the same time, the rhetorical use of its Global Compact "membership" goes against the spirit of transparency and improvement the Compact implies. Critics of the company are referred to their commitment to the Global Compact, as if that alone improved the company's record. After the *Multinational Monitor*, a U.S.-based monthly magazine, chose Bayer as one of the year's ten worst corporations of 2001 for its role regarding HIV drug pricing in the Third World, Bayer issued a statement, which said in part:

> Bayer rejects the accusations and defamations by the U.S.-based Multinational Monitor in its so-called "negative list" of the "Ten Worst Corporations of the Year 2001" published in December in the U.S. According to Multinational Monitor, the list includes companies that defraud the public, spoil the environment and neglect workers rights. Multinational Monitor is the organ of an alliance of activist groups that have the common aim of criticizing companies. It is no coincidence that this news was publicized by the so-called "Coalition against Bayer Dangers" shortly before Bayer's planned listing in the United States. The reasons Multinational Monitor provides for including Bayer on the list are one-sided and are exaggerated to describe alleged "scandals." This presentation fits into the agitation that the Coalition Against Bayer Dangers has pushed forward

against Bayer and its subsidiaries for years. . . . In 2001, Bayer was picked by U.S.-based magazine Fortune as one of the "most admired companies" in the United States. Bayer is one of the founding members of the U.N. Global Compact of U.N. Secretary Kofi Annan, which was started in July 2001. Therein the company obliges itself to agree with and spread nine principles the U.N. picked in the fields of human rights, social standards and environmental protection.[13]

Note the attempt to hide behind "membership" in the Global Compact. The U.N. has said, and Bayer is surely aware, that Global Compact participation does not imply a sign of approval from the U.N. However, the implication of association with Kofi Annan is clear. Bayer's statement does not address any of the substance of the *Multinational Monitor* article; rather it attacks company critics and hides behind the Global Compact.

Bluewash Snapshot #8: Eskom

One of the most influential companies on the continent, Eskom dominates the electricity supply industries of South and Southern Africa, generating over half the electricity produced in the whole of Africa. Eskom is a financial supporter of the Johannesburg Summit and influential in Business Action for Sustainable Development (see page 17).

Eskom says it is "embracing sustainable development," which is going to be quite difficult because the company is South Africa's largest greenhouse-gas emitter. Its primary fuel is coal, the fossil fuel with the highest carbon emissions per unit of output. Furthermore, coal is likely to remain its core business for the future. The emphasis on electricity from coal is difficult to reconcile with Principle Nine of the Global Compact, "encourage the development and diffusion of environmentally friendly technologies."

Eskom's number-two business is nuclear power, not a major contributor to global warming, but still the riskiest and most expensive power option. Nuclear power, because of the risk of accident and the lack of a solution for radioactive waste, is inherently contradictory to Global Compact Principle Seven, a precautionary approach to environmental challenges.

Historically, Eskom, an apartheid-era state company, has violated human rights through its discriminatory policies on access to electricity. The current process of privatization, along with charging poor customers more than they can afford, confronts the company with protests, and even strikes, by workers and community residents. Eskom still has some distance to go to abide fully by Global Compact Principle One, to "support and respect the protection of international human rights within [the company's] sphere of influence," and Principle Two, "make sure [they] are not complicit in human rights abuses."[14]

Afterword

It is not a foregone conclusion that the human race will be in a position to hold an Earth Summit III. If we are, UNEP, or whatever agency exists in 2012, is likely to report, again, that the environment has worsened, and that giant corporations as well as individual consumers must change their ways to save the planet. It doesn't have to be that way. The public is stirred up against excessive corporate power **now**, in favor of a more just system. It is a matter of time for governments to catch up. The longer it takes, the harder the changes will be, and the more damage we will have to live with.

As the most comprehensive intergovernmental organization, it is logical that the U.N. become the global nerve center of corporate accountability. But as the events recounted in this book make clear, that will not happen easily. Years of pressure on the U.N. to be business-friendly have pushed the world body into an almost supine position vis à vis international business. The U.N. will have to be dragged into becoming the preeminent institution of corporate accountability. "We the peoples" will have to do that dragging.

The U.N.'s embrace of corporate partnerships at the expense of accountability measures brought the conflict over corporate globalization into stark relief just in time for Johannesburg. As much as any factor, these perilous partnerships have left many who had high hopes for the Earth Summits with a sense of emptiness and failure.

As this book goes to press, scandalous and illegal corporate behavior is coming to light almost every day, undermining investor and general confidence in U.S. business and the stock market. The need for improved corporate accountability—even to shareholders—is becoming widely understood. That accountability must be extended to everyone affected by corporate behavior, and it must include not just financial but also social and environmental performance. The time is ripe, and the U.N. can have a role to play.

We the peoples can begin to change the balance of power at the United Nations. Through massive networks of NGOs, community groups, indigenous federations, labor unions, professional associations, friendly governments, academics, and more, we can form our own Compact with the U.N.—the Citizens Compact—dedicated to monitoring corporations and holding them accountable. We can study corporate behavior and submit our studies to the Global Compact Office, the Sub-Commission on Human Rights and other U.N. bodies. They may not welcome our submissions at first. Our studies may be closer to worst practices than best practices cases. Eventually, however, the overwhelming evidence of the need for corporate accountability will achieve a change; it must do so in order to save the planet.

Bringing cases and grievances to the United Nations is not a substitute for organizing and campaigning locally, nationally, globally and directly on corporations. That work continues and will continue. By integrating that work into global politics, by translating the growing desire for democracy and justice into political pressure at all levels, we may yet find the U.N. an ally in the effort to exert greater democratic control over corporations.

Notes

Preface

[1] Phyllis Bennis, *Calling the Shots*, New York: Olive Branch Press, 1996, 2000.

Chapter 1: The Globalization Decade

[1] "Poverty and the environment beached in Bali; will governments let us down in Johannesburg too?" statement signed by Consumers International, Danish 92 Group, Friends of the Earth International, Oxfam International, the World Wide Fund for Nature, and ANPED, Bali, June 7, 2002.

[2] "Bali Meeting Ends Without Agreement," UN Wire, United Nations Foundation, June 7, 2002.

[3] Arjun Makhijani, A. van Buren, A. Bickel, and S. Saleska, "Climate Change and Transnational Corporations Analysis and Trends," United Nations Centre on Transnational Corporations, Environment Series No.2, New York: United Nations, 1992 (47).

[4] Jed Greer and Kenny Bruno, *Greenwash: The Reality behind Corporate Environmentalism*, New York and Penang: Apex Press and Third World Network, 1996.

[5] U.N. Food and Agriculture Organization, *The State of the World's Fisheries and Aquaculture*, Rome: United Nations, 1995 (6).

[6] Roger Olsson, ed., *The Taiga: A Treasure—Or Timber and Trash?* 4th ed., Sokkmokk, Sweden: Taiga Rescue Network, 1993 (11).

7   Greenpeace International, Third World Network, Friends of the Earth International, and Brazilian Forum of NGOs, "A 10 Point Plan to Save the Earth Summit," Rio de Janeiro, March 1992; unpublished.

8   See Lori Wallach and Michelle Sforza, *Whose Trade Organization?*, Washington, D.C.: Public Citizen, October 1999.

9   Heinrich Boll Foundation, "The Jo'burg Memo," Berlin, April 2002 (12).

10 See, for example, Christopher Marquis, "Satisfied with UN Reforms, Helms Relents on Back Dues," *New York Times*, January 9, 2001.

11 United Nations Conference on Trade and Development, *World Investment Report 1994*, Geneva; United Nations Conference on Trade and Development, "Foreign Direct Investment Soars, But Will Decline This Year," press release, Geneva, September 18, 2001.

12 Institute for Policy Studies, "Top 200: The Rise of Corporate Global Power," report, December 2000.

13 "Multinationals and the World Trade Organisation," World Development Movement, London, September 1999.

14 According to the U.N.'s *World Investment Report 2000*, 99 of the 100 largest transnational corporations are from the industrialized countries (New York and Geneva, 11–13).

15 Renato Ruggiero, Director-General of the World Trade Organization, speech presented to the UNCTAD Trade and Development Board, October 8, 1996. Quoted on the Public Citizen website, www.citizen.org/trade/issues/mai/Investor/articles.cfm?ID=1096, accessed May 28, 2002.

16 Lori Wallach and Michelle Sforza, *Whose Trade Organization?*

17 Sarah Anderson, "Seven Years under NAFTA," Washington, D.C.: Institute for Policy Studies, January 2001.

18 Sarah Anderson, "Seven Years under NAFTA."

19 United Nations Conference on Trade and Development, *World Investment Report 1994*, Geneva; United Nations Conference on Trade and Development, "Foreign Direct Investment Soars, But Will Decline This Year," press release, Geneva, September 18, 2001.

20 United Nations, *World Investment Report 2000*, New York and Geneva, page 70.

21 Daphne Wysham and Jim Vallette, "Fueling Climate Change: Business as Usual?", Washington, D.C.: Institute for Policy Studies and Friends of the Earth, May 1999. See also www.seen.org.

22 See Chapters 1 and 5 of Joshua Karliner's *The Corporate Planet: Ecology and Politics in the Age of Globalization*, San Francisco: Sierra Club Books, 1997.

23 Mexico 2000 census figures, cited in Jerry Sanders, "Two Mexicos and Fox's Quandary," *The Nation*, February 26, 2001.

24 Sarah Anderson, "Seven Years Under NAFTA."

25 Walden Bello, "From Melbourne to Prague: The Struggle for a Deglobalized World," Bangkok: Focus on the Global South, September 6, 2000, www.focusweb.org.

26 *State of the World 2002: Special World Summit Edition*, Washington, D.C.: Worldwatch Institute, January 10, 2002.

27 *State of the World 2002: Special World Summit Edition.*

28 UNEP, "State of the Planet Is Getting Worse, but for Many It's Still 'Business as Usual,'" news release, Paris and Nairobi, May 15, 2002.

29 UNEP, "State of the Planet Is Getting Worse, but for Many It's Still 'Business as Usual.'"

30 See Kenny Bruno and Jed Greer, *Greenwash: The Reality behind Corporate Environmentalism*, New York and Penang: Apex Press and Third World Network, 1996; and Joshua Karliner, *The Corporate Planet*, Chapter 1.

31 See Jerry Mander and Edward Goldsmith (eds.), *The Case against the Global Economy*, San Francisco: Sierra Club Books, 1996.

32 Martin Khor, *Globalisation and the Crisis of Sustainable Development*, Penang: Third World Network, 2001 (37).

33 *State of the World 2002: Special World Summit Edition.*

34 *State of the World 2002: Special World Summit Edition.*

35 *State of the World 2002: Special World Summit Edition.*

36 Martin Khor, *Globalisation and the Crisis of Sustainable Development* (26–27).

37 Joshua Karliner, *The Corporate Planet: Ecology and Politics in the Age of Globalization* (13–29; 133–167).

38 Martin Khor, *Globalisation and the Crisis of Sustainable Development* (12–13).

39 See Kenny Bruno and Jed Greer, *Greenwash: The Reality behind Corporate Environmentalism*; and www.corpwatch.org/greenwash.

40 Letter from dozens of environment and development organizations and networks to Nitin Desai, United Nations Secretary General of the Johannesburg Summit and Under-Secretary General for Economic and Social Affairs, March 25, 2002. See text in Appendix C.

41 Stephan Schmidheiny with the Business Council for Sustainable Development, *Changing Course: A Global Business Perspective on Development and the Environment*, Cambridge, Mass.: The MIT Press, 1992 (201–202).

42 Stephen Kretzmann and Shannon Wright, *Human Rights and Environmental Operations Information on the Royal Dutch/Shell Group of Companies 1996-1997*, San Francisco: Project Underground and Rainforest Action Network, 1997 (5).

43 Bronwen Manby, "The Price of Oil," New York: Human Rights Watch, 1999.

44 Stephan Schmidkeiny with the Business Council for Sustainable Development, *Changing Course: A Global Business Perspective on Development and the Environment*, 202.

45 Quoted in Stephen Kretzmann and Shannon Wright, *Human Rights and Environmental Operations Information on the Royal Dutch/Shell Group of Companies: Independent Annual Report*, San Francisco: Project Underground and Rainforest Action Network, 1997.

46 Bob Herbert, "Unholy Alliance in Nigeria," op-ed, *New York Times*, January 26, 1996; transcript of "a testimony" by Dr. Owens Wiwa, brother of Ken Saro-Wiwa, undated, available on www.greenpeace.org/search.shtml.

47 Quoted in Joshua Hammer, "Nigeria Crude: A Hanged Man and an Oil-Fouled Landscape," *Harper's*, June 1996: 59.

48 Jennifer Davis, "Squeezing Apartheid," *Bulletin of the Atomic Scientists*, November 1993.

49 Kenny Bruno, Joshua Karliner and China Brotsky, *Greenhouse Gangsters vs. Climate Justice*, San Francisco: CorpWatch, November 1999.

50 Quoted in CorpWatch, "Shell's Climate Greenwash," press release, The Hague, November 20, 2000. www.corpwatch.org/press/PPD.jsp?articleid=925.

51 Royal Dutch Shell, "Cloud the Future or Clear the Air," advertisement, *Financial Times*, November 14, 2000.

52 Kenny Bruno, Joshua Karliner and China Brotsky, *Greenhouse Gangsters vs. Climate Justice*, San Francisco: CorpWatch, November 1999. See also Rick Heede, "Oil Industry and Climate Change," Amsterdam: Greenpeace International, 1998, from "Total Anthropogenic CO2 Emissions," Table 1 in Updated Information on Greenhouse Gas Emissions and Projections, subsidiary body for Implementation, Framework Convention on Climate Change, United Nations FCCC.SBI.ING 4/10/14.97 and "Emissions from Fossil Fuel Burning and Cement Manufacturing, 1995," Data Table 16.1 from Carbon Dioxide Information Analysis Center, reprinted in World Resources 1998–1999, New York: World Resources Institute, Oxford University Press, 1998.

53 Cited in "Rio + 10 and the Corporate Greenwash of Globalisation" *Corporate Europe Observer* 9 (June 2001).

54 CorpWatch, "NGOs to Monitor Business Group's Plans for Earth Summit II," press release, April 18, 2001. www.corpwatch.org /press/PPD.jsp?articleid=929.

55 Kofi Annan, "Working Together," *Business in Africa*, February 2000.

56 Kofi Annan, "Working Together."

57 Slogan of World Social Forum and "Another World Is Possible" Coalition.

Chapter 2: The Corporate Capture of the Rio Earth Summit

1 Cited in Joshua Karliner, *The Corporate Planet: Ecology and Politics in the Age of Globalization*, San Francisco: Sierra Club Books, 1997 (30). Several sections in this chapter draw from this book.

2 Vandana Shiva, "Transfer of Technology," Third World Network Briefing Papers for UNCED, August 1991.

3 Judith Richter, *Holding Corporations Accountable*, London and New York: Zed Books, 2001.

4 UNICEF webpage www.unicef.org/programme/nutrition/focus /infant.html, accessed April 19, 2002.

5 Judith Richter, *Holding Corporations Accountable*.

6 Judith Richter, *Holding Corporations Accountable*.

7   Commission on Transnational Corporations, "Transnational Corporations and Sustainable Development: Recommendations of the Executive Director," United Nations Economic and Social Council, January 1992, E/C.10/1992/2.

8   U.N., "UNCTAD Gets TNCs and Science/Technology Sectors," *Third World Economics*, April 1–15, 1993.

9   Cited in Tom Athanasiou, *Divided Planet: The Ecology of Rich and Poor*, Boston: Little, Brown, 1996 (199–200).

10 Stephan Schmidheiny with the Business Council for Sustainable Development, *Changing Course: A Global Business Perspective on Development and the Environment*, Cambridge, Mass.: The MIT Press, 1992.

11 Stephan Schmidheiny with BCSD, *Changing Course* (1–178).

12 Willums and Goluke, *From Ideas to Action* (87–88).

13 Marlise Simons, "Ecological Plea from Executives: International Group Urges Action at Rio," *New York Times*, May 8, 1992.

14 Thomas Harding, Danny Kennedy, Pratap Chatterjee, *Whose Summit Is It Anyway? An Investigative Report on the Corporate Sponsorship of the Earth Summit*, Rio de Janeiro: ASEED-International Youth Network, June 1992.

15 This section and the next draw on Chapter 2 of Joshua Karliner's *The Corporate Planet: Ecology and Politics in the Age of Globalization*, San Francisco: Sierra Club Books, 1997.

16 Martin Khor, *Globalisation and the Crisis of Sustainable Development*, Penang: Third World Network, 2001 (4).

17 Harris Gleckman, "Transnational Corporations Strategic Responses to 'Sustainable Development,'" in Helge Ole Bergesen, Georg Parmann and Oystein B. Thommessen (eds.), *Green Globe Year Book of International Cooperations in Environment and Development 1995*, New York: Oxford University Press (93–106).

18 "Business Charter for Sustainable Development," Paris: International Chamber of Commerce, 1991.

19 Tom Athanasiou, *Divided Planet: The Ecology of Rich and Poor*, Boston: Little, Brown, 1996 (282–286).

20 Daphne Wysham and Jim Vallette, "Fueling Climate Change: Business as Usual?", Washington, D.C.: Institute for Policy Studies and Friends of the Earth, May 1999. See also www.seen.org.

21 Third World Network, "Earth Summit Briefings," Penang; Greenpeace, "Beyond UNCED" Amsterdam; Greenpeace, "UNCED Undone: Key Issues Agenda 21 Doesn't Address," Amsterdam: Greenpeace International, March 1992; NGO Committee on Disarmament, Inc., "Toxic Militarism Should Be on UNCED's Agenda," *Disarmament Times: Special Double Issue, Militarism and the Environment* 15(1), March 1992; Angela Harkavy, "The Final Effort: A Progress Report on Preparatory Negotiations for UNCED," Washington, D.C.: National Wildlife Federation/CAPE '92, June 1992.

22 Harris Gleckman, "Transnational Corporations and Sustainable Development: Reflections from Inside the Debate," draft document, August 21, 1992; "Transnational Corporations and Sustainable Development: A Review of Agenda 21," New York: United Nations Transnational Corporations and Management Division, Department of Economic and Social Development, October 10, 1992.

23 Willums and Goluke, *From Ideas to Action* (20–21).

24 "Special Session of General Assembly on Implementation of Agenda 21 Concludes at Headquarters," press release Ga/9276 Env/Dev/442, June 23–27, 1997.

25 David Korten, "The United Nations and the Corporate Agenda," received from author via Internet, July 1997.

26 Corporate Europe Observatory, "Rio +10 and the Corporate Greenwash of Globalisation," *Corporate Europe Observer* 9 (June 2001).

27 Kenny Bruno and Jed Greer, *Greenwash: The Reality behind Corporate Environmentalism*, New York: Apex Press, 1996 (25).

28 Jim Vallette (ed.), "The International Trade in Wastes," Washington, D.C.: Greenpeace, 1990.

29 Basel Action Network, www.ban.org, accessed April 20, 2002.

30 "Exporting Harm—The High-Tech Trashing of Asia," Seattle and San Jose, Calif.: Basel Action Network and Silicon Valley Toxics Coalition, February 25, 2002.

31 Nityanand Jayaraman and Kenny Bruno, "Trading in Disaster—World Trade Center Scrap Lands in India," CorpWatch, February 6, 2002, www.corpwatch.org/issues/PID.jsp?articleid=1608.

[32] William K. Reilly, "Reflections on the Earth Summit," memorandum to all EPA employees (no date); see also Office of the Vice President, Memorandum for Bill Kristol, from John Cohressen and David McIntosh, "Major Problems with the Draft Convention of Biological Diversity," April 14, 1992.

[33] Cited in Kenny Bruno, "The Corporate Capture of the Earth Summit," *Multinational Monitor*, July/August 1992 (17).

[34] Jonathan Plaut, statement before the U.S. House of Representatives Committee on Foreign Affairs, July 21, 1992.

[35] William K. Reilly, testimony before the U.S. House of Representatives Committee on Foreign Affairs, July 28, 1992.

[36] Jane Rissler and Margaret Mellon, *Perils Amidst the Promise: Ecological Risks of Transgenic Crops in a Global Market*, Cambridge, Mass.: Union of Concerned Scientists, 1993.

[37] "U.S. Interpretive Statement Makes Mockery of Convention," *The Biodiversity Coalition Newsletter No. 7*, November 1993.

[38] Gurdial Singh Nijar, "The South Finally Secures a Biosafety Protocol," *Third World Resurgence* 65/66 (January/February 1996).

[39] Gurdial Singh Nijar, "CSD Staves Off U.S. Assault on Balanced Approach to Biotech" and "U.N. Accused of Industry Bias on Biotech," both in *Third World Resurgence* 58 (June 1995).

[40] Tony Clarke with Brenda Inouye, *Galloping Gene Giants*, Toronto: Polaris Institute, February 2002, (42).

[41] Tony Clarke with Brenda Inouye, *Galloping Gene Giants* (35).

[42] Andrew Pollack, "U.S. and Allies Block Treaty on Genetically Altered Goods," *The New York Times*, February 25, 1999.

[43] Corporate Europe Observatory, "Corporate Campaign to Corrupt the Kyoto Protocol Continues after COP-6," CorpWatch, www.corpwatch.org/campaigns/PRT.jsp?articleid=980.

[44] Corporate Europe Observatory, "Corporate Campaign to Corrupt the Kyoto Protocol Continues after COP-6."

Chapter 3: The Swoosh, the Shell and the Olive Branch

[1] Judith Richter, *Holding Corporations Accountable*, London and New York: Zed Books, 2001.

[2] See the CorpWatch website, www.corpwatch.org/campaigns /PCD.jsp?articleid=216, for a more in-depth treatment of this question.

3   Greenwash Award Earthday 2001: American Chemistry Council: www.corpwatch.org/campaigns/PCD.jsp?articleid=216.

4   Personal communication with David Roe, Senior Attorney with Environmental Defense, April 2001.

5   "Cooperation between the United Nations and Business: Joint Statement on Common Interests by the Secretary-General of the United Nations and the International Chamber of Commerce," *ICC Business World*, New York: International Chamber of Commerce, February 9, 1998.

6   "Cooperation between the United Nations and Business: Joint Statement on Common Interests by the Secretary-General of the United Nations and the International Chamber of Commerce."

7   Tyler Giannini et al., "Total Denial Continues," Chiang Mai and Washington, D.C.: EarthRights International, May 2000.

8   Fred Eckhard, "Highlights from the Noon Briefing," New York: Office of the Secretary General, U.N. Headquarters, July 20, 2000.

9   "U.N. and private sector need each other—Kofi Annan," *ICC Business World*, International Chamber of Commerce, September 23, 1998.

10 Letter from Under-Secretary General John Ruggie to authors et al., July 24, 2000, on file with authors.

11 Speech of UNICEF Executive Director Carol Bellamy to Harvard International Development Conference, Cambridge, Mass., April 16, 1999.

12 Interoffice memorandum from Elmi Watanabe, Assistant Administrator and Director, Bureau for Development Policy, UNDP, July 12, 1998.

13 "The Global Sustainable Development Facility: 2B2M," internal document, New York: The United Nations Development Programme, July 1998; Joshua Karliner, *A Perilous Partnership: The United Nations Development Programme's Flirtation with Corporate Collaboration*, San Francisco: CorpWatch/TRAC in collaboration with the Institute for Policy Studies and the Council on International and Public Affairs, March 16, 1999.

14 William Finnegan, "Leasing the Rain," *The New Yorker*, April 8, 2002.

15 "The Global Sustainable Development Facility: 2B2M."

16 Author attended this meeting between NGOs and UNDP staff in May of 1999.

[17] "Guidelines and Procedures for Mobilization of Resources from the Private Sector," New York: Division for Resources Mobilization, Bureau for Resources and External Affairs, UNDP, November 1998.

[18] "Guidelines and Procedures for Mobilization of Resources from the Private Sector."

[19] Personal communication with Georg Kell, Global Compact Executive Head, Spring 1999.

[20] Claudia H. Deutsch, "Unlikely Allies with the United Nations," New York Times, December 10, 1999 (C1).

[21] Smitu Kothari and Michelle Chawla (eds.), "UNDeePer in the Corporate Mire," New Delhi: Kalpavriksh et al., Publishers, February 2002.

[22] Smitu Kothari and Michelle Chawla (eds.), "UNDeePer in the Corporate Mire."

[23] The Business Humanitarian Forum, press release, Geneva, January 27, 1999.

[24] See www.aflcio.org/publ/press2002/pr0520.htm.

[25] Tyler Giannini et al., "Total Denial Continues."

[26] Doe et al. v. Unocal et al., Order Granting Defendants Motion for Summary Judgment, Judge Ronald S.W. Lew, filed August 31, 2000, U.S. Federal Court, Central District of California.

[27] Tyler Giannini et al., "Total Denial Continues."

[28] Business Humanitarian Forum, "Building Mutual Support Between Humanitarian Organization and the Business Community," undated report on January 27, 1999 meeting of the BHF; Conference Agenda, "Defining New Cooperation in the Humanitarian Agenda," November 1–2, 1999 Washington D.C., and letter from John Horekens, Director, Division of Communications and Information, UNHCR, to TRAC et al., Oct. 8, 1999, on file with authors.

[29] Kofi Annan, "Message to the Business Humanitarian Forum," Geneva, January 27, 1999.

[30] Kenny Bruno and Joshua Karliner, "Tangled Up in Blue," CorpWatch, September 2000.

31 "The U.S. in Haiti—How to Get Rich on 11 Cents an Hour," report produced for the National Labor Committee, January 1996; "Mickey Mouse Goes to Haiti: Walt Disney and the Science of Exploitation," video produced by National Labor Committee, New York, 1996; "An Appeal to Disney in Haiti," letter from Charles Kernaghan, Director of National Labor Committee, to Michael Eisner, CEO of Disney, May 29, 1996.

32 Kofi Annan, "A Compact for the New Century," speech given to the World Economic Forum, January 31, 1999.

33 'The Global Compact Corporate Leadership in the World Economy," paper distributed at UNA-USA briefing at the Church Center in New York, January 10, 2002.

34 John Ruggie, "Remarks on the Global Compact to the NGO Community," Geneva: United Nations, October 13, 2000, available at www.unglobalcompact.org/un/gc/unweb.nsf/content /ruggiengo.htm, accessed June 10, 2002.

35 "The Global Compact," www.un.org/partners/business/fs1.htm, accessed October 25, 1999. This version of the Global Compact preamble was subsequently removed from the Global Compact website.

36 "The Global Compact," www.un.org/partners/business/fs1.htm, accessed October 25, 1999. This version was subsequently removed from the Global Compact website.

37 Kofi Annan, "A Compact for the New Century."

38 "Taming Globalization," *The Washington Post*, August 7, 2000.

39 Martin Khor, speech to the Millennium Summit, September 6, 2000.

40 Jan-Olaf Willums and Ulrich Goluke, *From Ideas to Action*, Oslo: International Chamber of Commerce, 1992 (9).

41 Global Compact website, www.unglobalcompact.org/un/gc /unweb.nsf/content/network.htm, accessed May 21, 2002.

42 Corporate Europe Observatory, "High Time for U.N. to Break 'Partnership' with the ICC," CorpWatch, available at www.corpwatch.org/campaigns/PCD.jsp?articleid+618, July 25, 2001.

43 "Business Leaders Advocate a Stronger United Nations and Take Up Challenge of Secretary-General's Global Compact," July 5, 1999. www.un.org/partners/business/iccun1.htm, accessed November 18, 1999.

44 Kofi Annan, "Address to the Chamber of Commerce of the United States of America," Washington D.C., June 8, 1999.

45 Corporate Europe Observatory, "High Time for U.N. to Break 'Partnership' with the ICC."

46 In 1998, ICC head Maucher of Nestlé announced in the *International Herald Tribune*: "We have established the ICC as the preferred dialogue partner for business with the United Nations and other international institutions." Quoted in Judith Richter, *Holding Corporations Accountable*. See also Corporate Europe Observatory, "High Time for U.N. to Break 'Partnership' with the ICC."

47 Maria Livianos Cattaui, "Yes to Annan's 'Global Compact' If It Isn't a License to Meddle," *International Herald Tribune*, July 26, 2000.

48 Statement of Amnesty International's Pierre Sane to the Global Compact meeting, July 26, 2000.

49 ICAP webpage, www.icap.org/international/global_compact.html, accessed April 9, 2002.

50 When CorpWatch pointed out that ICAP was, in fact, representing business interests, the Global Compact Office agreed to move ICAP to the Business category. Six weeks later, as this book went to press, that change had not been made to the Global Compact website, www.unglobalcompact.org/un/gc/unweb.nsf/content/actors.htm, accessed May 23, 2002.

51 *U.N. 2000—Millennium Summit*, New York: United Nations September 6–8, 2000.

52 "Guidelines: Cooperation between the United Nations and the Business Community," New York: United Nations, July 17, 2000.

53 "Guidelines: Cooperation between the United Nations and the Business Community."

54 Question to Maria Eitel, Vice President of Nike, Global Compact press conference, U.N. Headquarters, July 26th, 2000, webcast at www.un.globalcompact.org; Pacifica Radio's *Democracy Now*, July 27, 2000.

55 Global Compact website, www.unglobalcompact.org/un/gc/unweb.nsf/content/network.htm.

56 "The Global Compact—What It Is and What It Isn't," New York: U.N. Global Compact Office, January 17, 2001.

57 Global Compact website, www.unglobalcompact.org/un/gc/unweb.nsf/content/learning.htm, accessed January10, 2002.

58 Peter Utting, *Business Responsibility for Sustainable Development*, Geneva: UNRISD, 2000 (11–12).

59 John Ruggie, "The Global Compact as Learning Network" Global Compact website, www.unglobalcompact.org/un/gc /unweb.nsf/content/JRuggie.htm, accessed May 22 2002.

60 "What Is BASD," from BASD website, www.basd-action.net/about/index.shtml, accessed December 11, 2001.

61 "Industry's Rio + 10 Strategy: Banking on Feel-good PR," Corporate Europe Observatory, Amsterdam December 2001.

62 Tyler Giannini et al., *Total Denial Continues*, Chiang Mai and Washington, D.C.: EarthRights International, May 2000.

63 "Business Award of the ICC in collaboration with UNEP," announcement on UNEP website, wwww.unepie.org/outreach /business/award.htm, accessed May 22, 2002.

Chapter 4: Corporate Accountability in the Twenty-First Century

1 "Who to Blame Ten Years after Rio: The Role of the U.S., Canada and Australia in Undermining the Rio Agreements," Amsterdam: Greenpeace International, January 2002.

2 "NGOs Refine Ways to Go after Big Oil," *Petroleum Intelligence Weekly*, April 29, 2002.

3 Danny Hakim, "Talking Green vs. Making Green," *The New York Times*, March 28, 2002.

4 Matthias Herfeldt, "Corporate-Driven Globalization: The Role of the World Economic Forum," Earth Times News Service, January 28, 2002. www.earthtimes.org/jan/ngoopinioncorporate jan28_02.htm, accessed May 23, 2002.

5 Edith Lederer, "UN: Swedish Businessman Loses Job," Associated Press, March 1, 2002.

6 Personal communication with David Waskow of Friends of the Earth, who attended a briefing with State Department officials in March 2002.

7 Wolfgang Sachs, "Environment and Development: The Story of a Dangerous Liaison," *The Ecologist* 21(6): 252–257 (1991).

8 Jack Freeman, "The other bomb: Lagging efforts to deal with population and progress," Earth Times News Service, June 7, 1998.

9 Testimony before the Committee on Resources, Subcommittee on Energy and Mineral Resources, U.S. House of Representatives,

presented by Laura E. Skaer, Executive Director, Northwest Mining Association, September 11, 1999, www.nwma.org/pdf /testimon.PDF+%22Poverty+is+the+worst+polluter%22&hl=en, accessed April 14, 2002.

10 "The Secretary–General—Message to the World Social Forum," delivered by Jose Antonio Ocampo, Executive Secretary of ECLAC, Porto Alegre, 4 February 2002.

11 See Mark Vallianatos, "License to Loot," Washington, D.C.: Friends of the Earth, 1998.

12 J. Oloka-Onyango and Deepika Udyama, "The Realization of Economic, Social and Cultural Rights: Globalization and its impact on the full enjoyment of human rights," Geneva: U.N. Subcommission on the Promotion and Protection of Human Rights, August 2000.

13 J. Oloka-Onyango and Deepika Udyama, "The Realization of Economic, Social and Cultural Rights: Globalization and its impact on the full enjoyment of human rights."

14 David Weissbrodt, "Principles relating to the human rights conduct of companies," working paper prepared for the Commission on Human Rights Sub-Commission on the Promotion and Protection of Human Rights, Item 4, 52nd session, May 2, 2000.

15 Joshua Karliner, "A Perilous Partnership," San Francisco: Transnational Resource & Action Center, March, 1999 (9).

16 See www.corpwatch.org/un.

Chapter 5: One Wash, Two Wash, Greenwash, Bluewash

1 Additional and more in-depth greenwash case studies are also available in *Greenwash: The Reality behind Corporate Environmentalism* and on the CorpWatch website: www.corpwatch.org/greenwash.

2 The Global Compact case studies here are excerpted from longer articles originally posted on www.corpwatch.org/un.

Chapter 6: Greenwash Snapshots

1 Carol Alexander, "Natural Gas: Bridging Fuel or Roadblock to Clean Energy?", Amsterdam: Greenpeace International, 1993.

2 Personal communication with Shannon Wright, Rainforest Action Network, June 2000.

3   BP press release, "BP Amoco Invests $45 Million in Solarex Stake to Create World's Biggest Solar Company," April 6, 1999.

4   BP press release, "BP Amoco and ARCO in $26.8 Billion Deal Agreed by Boards of Both Companies," April 1, 1999.

5   Greenpeace, "BP runs to courts to prevent Greenpeace ship from protecting the climate," press release, August 9, 2000.

6   "UK: Oil Giant BP Stops Political Donations," Associated Press, February 28, 2002.

7   David Barboza, "Farmers Are Scaling Back Genetically Altered Crops," *New York Times*, April 1, 2000 (A6).

8   David Barboza, "Industry Moves to Defend Biotechnology," *New York Times*, April 4, 2000 (C6).

9   See, for example, the Council for Biotechnology Information's website articles www.whybiotech.com/index.asp?id=1648 and www.whybiotech.com/index.asp?id=1285.

10 See Kenny Bruno, "Monsanto's Failing PR Strategy," *The Ecologist* 28(5) (September/October 1998).

11 Lewis C. Winters, "Does It Pay to Advertise to Hostile Audiences with Corporate Advertising?", *Journal of Advertising Research*, June–July 1988 (11–18).

12 Justin Lowe, "Chevron's Fish Stories," *San Francisco Bay Guardian*, July 18, 1990 (26).

13 Greg Lyon, *Target Four Investigation of Chevron Advertisements*, KRON-TV news video, San Francisco.

14 Cited in Justin Lowe and Hillary Hansen, "A Look behind the Advertising," *Earth Island Journal*, Winter 1990 (27).

15 Greg Lyon, *Target Four Investigation of Chevron Advertisements*.

16 Greg Lyon, *Target Four Investigation of Chevron Advertisements*.

17 Lewis C. Winters, "Does It Pay to Advertise to Hostile Audiences with Corporate Advertising?" *Journal of Advertising Research*, June–July 1988 (11–18).

18 Candace Morey et al., "Pollution Lineup," Cambridge, Mass.: Union of Concerned Scientists, March 2000 (2).

19 Michael Renner, "Rethinking the Role of the Automobile," WorldWatch Paper #84, 1988.

[20] "World Medical Association Statement on Traffic Injury," adopted by the 42nd World Medical Assembly, Rancho Mirage, Calif., October 1990, available at www.wma.net/e/policy/10-a_e.html, accessed June 12, 2002.

[21] Joshua Karliner and Kenny Bruno, "Ford's Earth Day Greenwash," *San Francisco Chronicle*, April 21, 2000.

[22] Personal communication with John Stauber, editor, *PR Watch*, May 20, 2002.

[23] "Earth Day 2000: How to Save the Earth and the Heroes for the Planet Who Are Making It Happen," *Time Special Edition*, Spring 2000.

[24] Candace Morey et al., "Pollution Lineup."

[25] Danny Hakim, "Talking Green vs. Making Green," *New York Times*, March 28, 2002 (C1).

[26] Serge Dedina and Emily Young, "Conservation and Development in the Gray Whale Lagoons of Baja California Sur, Mexico," Final Report to the U.S. Marine Mammal Commission, October 1995.

[27] Mark J. Spalding, "Laguna San Ignacio Briefing Book," prepared for Natural Resources Defense Council and International Fund for Animal Welfare, January 1998.

[28] Serge Dedina, *Saving the Gray Whale: People, Politics and Conservation in Baja California*, Tucson: University of Arizona Press, 2000 (83).

[29] For more on this story see Serge Dedina, *Saving the Gray Whale: People, Politics and Conservation in Baja California*.

[30] Monsanto 1996 Environmental Review, St. Louis, Mo.

[31] Monsanto 1996 Environmental Review.

[32] Peter Montague, "Milk, rBGH, and Biotechnology," *Rachels Hazardous Waste News #381*, published by Environmental Research Foundation, Annapolis.

[33] Peter Montague, "Making Milk: Basic Choices," *Rachel's Hazardous Waste News #384*, April 7, 1994.

34 Canola, like soya, is for oil used in a wide variety of processed foods not available to the world's hungry. For all of these "Roundup Ready" crops, the main advantage is ease of use for large-scale farmers that also wish to use Monsanto's Roundup herbicide. The main purpose is not to increase yield, and the premium price of the genetically engineered seeds puts it out of the reach of most small-scale farmers, especially in the Third World. See Mary Ellen McDonagh, "Biotechnology: Not an Answer to Hunger," available at www.bvmcong.org/salt/salt/spring2001/mcdonagh.htm.

35 CEO letter, Monsanto 1995 Environmental Review, St. Louis, Mo.

36 Reproduced in Jed Greer and Kenny Bruno, "Greenwash: The Reality behind Corporate Enivronmentalism," Third World Network, Penang, 1996 (212).

37 "Better Business Bureau: Nuclear Industry Ads 'Inaccurate,'" Public Citizen press release, December 9, 1998; and "Public Citizen Asks FTC to Declare NEI Ads False, Misleading," Public Citizen press release, June 2, 1999.

38 Katharine Q. Seelye, "After Lobbying, Nuclear Industry Finds Itself Back on Political Map," *New York Times*, May 23, 2001.

39 Amory B. Lovins, Rocky Mountain Institute (Colorado), "Why Nuclear Power's Failure in the Marketplace Is Irreversible (Fortunately for Nonproliferation and Climate Protection)," briefing paper presented at "Nuclear Power and Nuclear Weapons: Can We Have One without the Other?" Washington, D.C.: Nuclear Control Institute, April 2001.

40 Amory B. Lovins, Rocky Mountain Institute (Colorado), "Why Nuclear Power's Failure in the Marketplace is Irreversible (Fortunately for Nonproliferation and Climate Protection)."

41 WHO Slams Big Tobacco's Global Tactics," Associated Press, Geneva August 2, 2000, available at www.cbsnews.com/stories/2000/08/02/tech/main220936.shtml.

42 "Tobacco Companies' Strategies to Undermine Tobacco Control Activities at the World Health Organization—Report of the Committee of Experts on Tobacco Industry Documents," World Health Organization, July 2000; Gordon Fairchlough, "Cigarette Firms Tried to Foil WHO, Say Investigators," *Wall Street Journal*, August 2000.

[43] Opening remarks of Gro Harlem Brundtland, Director General, World Health Organisation, to Intergovernmental Negotiating Body on the WHO Framework Convention on Tobacco Control—Fourth Session, www.who.int/director-general/speeches /2002/english/20020318_inb4.html, accessed May 27, 2002.

[44] John A. Byrne, "Philip Morris; Inside America's Most Reviled Company," *Business Week Online*, November 29, 1999, available at www.businessweek.com/1999/99_48/b3657003.htm.

[45] Infact, "Harris Poll Confirms Active Support for Boycott of Philip Morris: Public Is Rejecting Image Makeover by Kraft's Parent Company," press release, February 7, 2002.

[46] John P. Pierce, "Smoking Initiation by Adolescent Girls, 1944 through 1988, an Association with Targeted Advertising," *Journal of the American Medical Association*, February 23, 1994 (610).

[47] Kelly Anderson and Tami Gold, 2001.

[48] Personal communication by authors with spokesperson Laurie Guzzinati of Philip Morris, February 14, 2001.

[49] Fortune 500 listings for the year 2000, www.fortune.com, accessed March 2001.

[50] "Leading National Advertisers," chart, *Ad Age*, September 25, 2000.

[51] For CCPA, see www.eren.doe.gov/climatechallenge /cc_accordxSOUTHRNC.htm; "Southern Company launches largest corporate electric vehicle lease program in nation," press release, March 31, 1999.

[52] "Benchmarking Air Emissions of the 100 Largest Electricity Generation Owners in the U.S."

[53] Ranking by 1995 Emissions of SO2, NRDC chart, available at www.nrdc.org/air/energy/utilprof/so2table.asp, accessed May 16, 2002, and Ranking by 1995 Emissions of Nox, NRDC chart, available at www.nrdc.org/air/energy/utilprof/noxtable.asp.

[54] Rick Heede, "Oil Industry and Climate Change," Amsterdam: Greenpeace International, 1998 (Appendix 5, page 61), from Table 1, "Total Anthropogenic CO2 Emission," updated information on greenhouse gas emissions and projections, Subsidiary Body for Implementation, Framework Convention on Climate Change, United Nations FCCC/SBI.INF 4/10/14/97 and Data Table 16.1, "Emissions from Fossil Fuel Burning and Cement Manufacturing, 1995," Carbon Dioxide Information Analysis Center, reprinted in *World Resources 1909-1999*, New York: World Resources Institute/Oxford University Press, 1998.

Chapter 7: Bluewash Snapshots

1 Global Compact website, www.unglobalcompact.org/un/gc /unweb.nsf/content/actors.htm, accessed May 24, 2002.

2 For a more in-depth treatment of Aventis's actions, see Gabriela Flora, Institute for Agriculture and Trade Policy, "Aventis: Global Compact Violator," CorpWatch Special Series, June 14, 2001. www.corpwatch.org/campaigns/PCD.jsp?articleid=621.

3 For a more in-depth treatment of Nike's behavior, see Tim Connor, Global Exchange, "Still Waiting for Nike to Respect the Right to Organize," CorpWatch Special Series, June 28, 2001. www.corpwatch.org/campaigns/PCD.jsp?articleid=619; and Tim Connor, "Still Waiting for Nike to Do It," San Francisco: Global Exchange, May 2001.

4 For a more in-depth treatment of issues surrounding Rio Tinto's Kelian gold mine, see Danny Kennedy, Project Underground, "Rio Tinto: Global Compact Violator: PT Kelian: A Case Study of Global Operations," CorpWatch Special Series, July 13, 2001. www.corpwatch.org/campaigns/PCD.jsp?articleid=622. See also Asia-Pacific Human Rights Network, "Associating with the Wrong Company: Rio Tinto's Record and the Global Compact," *Human Rights Features,* July 13, 2001, republished on CorpWatch at www.corpwatch.org/campaigns/PCD.jsp?articleid=623.

5 For a more in-depth treatment see Corporate Europe Observatory, "High Time for UN to Break 'Partnership' with the ICC," CorpWatch Special Series, July 25, 2001. www.corpwatch.org /campaigns/PCD.jsp?articleid=618.

6 For a more in-depth treatment see Nityanand Jayaraman, "Unilever's Mercury Fever," CorpWatch Special Series, October 4, 2001. www.corpwatch.org/campaigns/PCD.jsp?articleid=624.

7 For a more in-depth treatment see Nityanand Jayaraman, "Norsk Hydro: Global Compact Violator," CorpWatch Special Series, October 18, 2001. www.corpwatch.org/campaigns/PCD.jsp? articleid=620.

8 Philipp Mimkes, "Bayer and the Global Compact—How a Major Chemical and Pharmaceutical Company Greenwashes Its Image," Coalition Against Bayer Dangers, CorpWatch Special Series, July 2002, available at www.corpwatch.org/un.

9 Philipp Mimkes, "Bayer and the Global Compact—How a Major Chemical and Pharmaceutical Company Greenwashes Its Image."

10 The U.N. says that the Global Compact does not have members; the term "founding member" is used by Bayer and refers to their presence at the July 2000 launch event of the Compact in New York.

11 Philipp Mimkes, "Bayer and the Global Compact—How a Major Chemical and Pharmaceutical Company Greenwashes Its Image."

12 Global Compact website, www.unglobalcompact.org/un/gc /unweb.nsf/content/actors.htm

13 Statement by Bayer, printed in Letters Section, *Multinational Monitor* 23(1–2) (January/February 2002). Translated from the German by the Coalition Against Bayer Dangers.

14 Bryan Ashe, Earthlife Africa e Thekwini, "The Social and Ecological Footprint of South Africa's Power Utility," CorpWatch Special Series, July 2002, available at www.corpwatch.org/un.

Global Compact Principles and Participants

The Principles

Human Rights

The Secretary-General asked world business to

PRINCIPLE 1: support and respect the protection of international human rights within their sphere of influence; and

PRINCIPLE 2: make sure their own corporations are not complicit in human rights abuses.

Labour

The Secretary-General asked world business to uphold

PRINCIPLE 3: freedom of association and the effective recognition of the right to collective bargaining;

PRINCIPLE 4: the elimination of all forms of forced and compulsory labour;

PRINCIPLE 5: the effective abolition of child labour; and

PRINCIPLE 6: the elimination of discrimination in respect of employment and occupation.

Environment

The Secretary-General asked world business to

PRINCIPLE 7:   support a precautionary approach to environmental challenges;

PRINCIPLE 8:   undertake initiatives to promote greater environmental responsibility; and

PRINCIPLE 9:   encourage the development and diffusion of environmentally friendly technologies.

The Participants

- Labor and Civil Society Organizations Supporting the Global Compact
- The International Confederation of Free Trade Unions
- Amnesty International
- Lawyers Committee for Human Rights
- Human Rights Watch
- The World Conservation Union
- World Wide Fund for Nature
- World Resource Institute
- International Institute for Environment and Development

Regional International Networking Group

Business Associations Supporting the Global Compact

- International Chamber of Commerce
- International Organization of Employers
- World Business Council on Sustainable Development
- Prince of Wales Business Leaders Forum
- Business for Social Responsibility

Companies Participating in the Global Compact

There are two requirements for participation in the Global Compact: a letter of intent from the company CEO to the Secretary General, and the annual submission of efforts undertaken to advance the Compact's nine principles. The list below provides the names of the companies that fulfilled these requirements in 2001.

ABB
Aluminium Bahrain
Amazon Caribbean Guyana
Aracruz
Aventis
BASF
Bayer AG
BMW
Bohica Medical (SME—Australia)
BP
BT
Business Research & Development
   Initiative
Cargo Lifter AG
China Petroleum and Chemical
   Corporation
Cisco Systems
Credit Suisse Group
DaimlerChrysler
Deloitte Touche Tohmatsu
Deutsche Bank
Deutsche Telekom
DuPont
Electricité de France (EDF)
Ericsson
Eskom
Esquel
France Telecom
Gerling Group
Hindustan Organic Chemicals Ltd.
H&M Hennes & Mauritz AB
Indian Oil Corporation
ISS
Junyao Group
Ketchum
Kikkoman Corporation
LUCITÀ
Martha Tilaar Group
Morley Fund Managment

PT Mega Kelola Promoindo (SME—
   Indonesia)
National Thermal Power Corporation
Natura Cosméticos S/A
Nexen
Nike
Nogatec International
Novartis
Now for Future Pty Ltd
Organizaçöes Globo
Pearson plc
Placer Dome
Power Finance Corporation
PT Mega Kelola Promoindo
Pulsar Informatica Ltd.
Regis Engineering (SME—Tanzania)
Reputation Qest
Rio Tinto
SAP
Serendip Productions (SME—
   Pakistan)
Shell International Ltd.
Skanska AB
Ssovitex Design (SME—Uganda)
Standard Chartered Bank
Statoil
ST Microelectronics
Storebrand
Suez
Tata Iron and Steel Company
Telenor ASA
Translation City
Transnational Supply & Service
Trimtab Management Systems
UBS AG
Unilever
Volvo
William E. Connor & Associates
Yawal System (SME—Poland)

For the U.N.'s perspective on the Global Compact, see
www.unglobalcompact.org/

Citizens Compact on the United Nations and Corporations

Preamble

In January 1999, United Nations Secretary General Kofi Annan called for a "Global Compact" between the U.N. and the business community. In that Compact, he challenged business leaders to embrace and enact nine core principles derived from U.N. agreements on labor standards, human rights and environmental protection. In exchange, he promised, the U.N. will support free trade and open markets.

Citizen organizations and movements recognize that the private sector has enormous influence on human health, environment, development and human rights. Everyone shares the hope that economic well-being will bring real human development and ecological security. Yet as UNICEF Executive Director Carol Bellamy has said, "It is dangerous to assume that the goals of the private sector are somehow synonymous with those of the United Nations because they most emphatically are not." At times corporations work at cross purposes to the wider realization of rights and responsibilities enshrined in United Nations covenants, declarations and agreements.

The growing concentration of wealth and power in the hands of fundamentally undemocratic global corporations and other institutions of globalization with no accountability to governments or peoples is in direct conflict with the principles and aims of the United Nations to enhance human dignity and the capacity for self-governance. As the U.N. Sub-Commission on Human Rights puts it, the U.N. should not support institutions or corporations whose activities "create benefits for a small privileged minority at the expense of an increasingly disenfranchised majority."

Citizen organizations and movements support the mission and values of the United Nations. These objectives must have primacy of place and must not be subordinated to commercial trade, investment and finance rules. The U.N., as an institution that prioritizes human rights, health, labor standards, sustainable development and ecological protection over commercial interests, must have the capacity to exercise its mandate.

Citizen organizations and movements recognize that declining financial support from governments to the U.N. and its specialized agencies make their job harder. The U.N. must adjust to these circumstances; however it must do so while adhering to its Charter and its impartiality, and without compromising its commitment to its fundamental principles.

We propose a compact between the U.N. and civil society, regarding the U.N.'s relationship with the private sector. With this compact, we pledge our active support for a strengthening of the United Nations, financially and politically. Adherence to these nine principles will safeguard the image, mission and credibility of the United Nations as it deals with the private sector.

The Principles

1. Multinational corporations are too important for their conduct to be left to voluntary and self-generated standards. A legal framework, including monitoring, must be developed to govern their behavior on the world stage.

2. The United Nations will continue to develop tools to ensure universal values of environmental protection and human rights, through such mechanisms as multilateral environmental and human rights agreements, codes of marketing and ILO conventions.

3. The United Nations recognizes the legitimate purpose of national and local legislation to protect ecosystems, human

health, labor standards and human rights. The United Nations will assist civil society and governments in enacting and implementing such legislation.

4. The U.N. must find ways to ensure that other intergovernmental bodies, such as the IMF, World Bank and WTO, do not depart from the principles and goals of the U.N. Charter.

5. United Nations agencies will advise and offer assistance to corporations wishing to understand and improve their human rights and environmental behavior. Such assistance will not be considered a "partnership."

6. The United Nations does not endorse or promote products or brand names of any private corporation, and will avoid the appearance of such endorsements.

7. The United Nations will avoid any public association or financial relationship with companies with destructive practices, or products that are harmful to human health or the environment. Before entering any relationship with a corporation, the U.N. will thoroughly evaluate whether the objectives of that company are compatible with those of the U.N. In doing so, it must set up open and transparent processes of dialogue with NGOs and community groups with expertise on those corporations' activities.

8. The United Nations and its agencies will continue to fulfill their mission with funding from governments. In cases where private corporations wish to make a donation, the money will go to programs that have no connection to commercial projects for that company.

9. The U.N. will act with full transparency in all its dealings with the private sector, at the conceptual, planning and implementation stages. NGOs should have access to the same information in this regard as the private sector.

Partial list of groups endorsing the Citizens Compact and/or opposing the Global Compact

- Berne Declaration (Switzerland)
- BAYERwatch (Germany)
- Brazilian Institute of Economic and Social Analysis
- Centro de Derechos Humanos y Medio Ambiente (Argentina)
- Chile Sustentable (Chile)

- Corporate Europe Observatory (Netherlands)
- CorpWatch (U.S.)
- Ecoropa (France)
- Environmental Rights Action / Friends of the Earth (Nigeria)
- Essential Action (U.S.)
- Food First / Institute for Food and Development Policy (U.S.)
- Friends of the Earth (England, Wales and Northern Ireland)
- Global Exchange (U.S.)
- Greenpeace International (The Netherlands)
- Institute for Agriculture and Trade Policy (U.S.)
- Institute for Policy Studies (U.S.)
- International Baby Food Action Network (Switzerland and International)
- International Forum on Globalization (U.S.)
- International NGO Committee on Human Rights in Trade and Investment (India)
- International Rivers Network (U.S.)
- International South Group Network (Zimbabwe)
- Lokayan and International Group for Grassroots Initiatives (India)
- Movimiento Autoridades Indígenas de Colombia (Colombia)
- Movement for the Survival of the Ogoni People (MOSOP) (Nigeria)
- Organic Consumers Association (U.S.)
- Program on Corporations, Law and Democracy (U.S.)
- Project Underground (U.S.)
- Rural Advancement Foundation International (Canada)
- South Asia Network on Dams, Rivers and People (India)
- Tebtebba Foundation (The Philippines)
- Third World Network (Malaysia)
- Transnational Institute (Netherlands)
- Women's Environment and Development Network (U.S.)
- Third World Institute (Uruguay)

Alliance for a Corporate-Free U.N.: Description and Letters to Kofi Annan and Nitin Desai

The Alliance for a Corporate-Free U.N. is a global network of human rights, environment and development groups working to address undue corporate influence in the United Nations and to support U.N. initiatives to hold corporations accountable on issues of human rights, labor rights and the environment. CorpWatch serves as the Alliance secretariat.

Platform

The members of the Alliance believe in a United Nations which

- holds commercial rules subservient to human rights, labor and environmental principles
- avoids excessive and undue corporate influence
- holds corporations accountable in a legal framework
- maintains integrity of international social and environmental agreements
- receives adequate funding from governments

Activities

The Alliance has three main activities:

- monitoring and exposing corporate partnerships and undue corporate influence at the U.N.
- making action to pressure the U.N. to avoid such partnerships and influence
- promoting and supporting U.N.-related measures to hold corporations accountable

Steering Committee

CorpWatch (U.S.)—Secretariat

Corporate Europe Observatory (Netherlands)

Council on International and Public Affairs (U.S.)

Brazilian Institute for Social and Economic Analysis (Brazil)

Focus on the Global South (Thailand)

Institute for Policy Studies (U.S.)

International Baby Food Action Network (Switzerland/International)

International NGO Committee on Human Rights in Trade and Investment (India)

Tebtebba Foundation, Inc. (Philippines)

Third World Institute (Uruguay)

Third World Network (Malaysia)

Women's Environment and Development Organization (U.S.)

Letters

This letter to Kofi Annan was sent by members of the Alliance for a Corporate-Free U.N. a few days before the launch of the Global Compact.

July 20, 2000

His Excellency Mr. Kofi Annan
Secretary General
Room 3800
United Nations, NY 10017

Mr. Secretary General,

We write to you as individuals who care deeply about the
United Nations and on behalf of organizations that have
worked for years to strengthen and support it.

We are writing to express our concern and reservations
about the Global Compact.

On the one hand, we recognize the importance of bringing
business behavior in line with the universal values and
standards represented by the nine principles of the Global
Compact.

However, there are two aspects of the Global Compact that
trouble us. First, the text implies a universal consensus that
open markets are the primary force for development. As you
are aware, there is intense debate over the benefits and
harms of free trade and market liberalization as currently
promoted by the WTO and other institutions.

Many sectors of society do not concur with the Global
Compact's vision of advancing popular social values "as part
and parcel of the globalization process," to "ensure that
markets remain open." Many do not agree with the
assumption of the Global Compact that globalization in its
current form can be made sustainable and equitable, even if
accompanied by the implementation of standards for human
rights, labor and the environment.

We recognize that corporate-driven globalization has
significant support among governments and business.
However, that support is far from universal. Your support
for this ideology, as official U.N. policy, has the effect of
delegitimizing the work and aspirations of those sectors that
believe that an unregulated market is incompatible with
equity and environmental sustainability.

Our second concern is the purely voluntary nature of the
Global Compact, and the lack of monitoring and

enforcement provisions. We are well aware that many corporations would like nothing better than to wrap themselves in the flag of the United Nations in order to "bluewash" their public image, while at the same time avoiding signficant changes to their behavior. The question is how to get them to abide by the principles in the Global Compact.

Without monitoring, the public will be no better able to assess the behavior, as opposed to the rhetoric, of corporations. Without independent assessment, the interpretation of whether a company is abiding by the Global Compact's principles or not will be left largely to the company itself.

Many of the corporations being asked to endorse the Global Compact suggest that while corporations SHOULD be responsible, efforts by governments to hold corporations accountable to international values and standards are harmful to development, innovation and human progress. Many in the NGO community reject this premise. On the contrary, we stress that markets cannot allocate fairly and efficiently without clear and impartially enforced rules, established through open, democractic processes. Asking corporations, many of which are repeat offenders of both the law and commonly accepted standards of responsibility, to endorse a vague statement of commitment to human rights, labor and environmental standards, draws attention away from the need for more substantial action to hold corporations accountable for their behavior.

As you are aware, the U.N. Subcomission on the Promotion and Protection of Human Rights is currently drafting a legal instrument on TNCs and human rights. We would look for your support for this initiative.

Although it may take years before we can hope to achieve a binding legal framework for the transnational behavior of business in the human rights, environmental and labor realms, we believe it is necessary to start down that road, and to begin building the political support for that goal now. Therefore, the undersigned groups respectfully request you to reassess the Global Compact, taking into account the concerns above.

In addition, we offer an alternative, the Citizens Compact, for your consideration. The Citizens Compact stresses the importance of a legal framework for corporate behavior in the global economy. The Citizens Compact also provides suggested guidelines for interactions between the UN and the private sector.

We invite your comments on the Citizens Compact and hope you will consider endorsing it.

Again, we believe that bringing corporate behavior in line with the universal principles and values of the United Nations is a goal of extremely high importance. We look forward to working with you and the entire United Nations system toward that goal.

Sincerely,

Upendra Baxi, Professor of Law, University of Warwick U.K. and former Vice Chancellor, University of Delhi (India)

Roberto Bissio, Third World Institute (Uruguay)

Thilo Bode, Executive Director, Greenpeace International (Netherlands)

Walden Bello, Director, Focus on the Global South (Thailand)

John Cavanagh, Director, Institute for Policy Studies (U.S.)

Susan George, Associate Director, Transnational Institute (Netherlands)

Olivier Hoedemen, Corporate Europe Observatory (Netherlands)

Joshua Karliner, Executive Director, CorpWatch (U.S.)

Martin Khor, Director, Third World Network (Malaysia)

Miloon Kothari, Coordinator, International NGO Committee on Human Rights in Trade and Investment (India)

Smitu Kothari, President, International Group for Grassroots Initiatives (India)

Sara Larrain, Coordinator, Chile Sustentable (Chile)

Jerry Mander, Director, International Forum on Globalization (U.S.)

Ward Morehouse, Director, Program on Corporations, Law and Democracy (U.S.)

Atila Roque, Programme Coordinator, Brazilian Institute of Economic and Social Analysis (Brazil)

Elisabeth Sterken, National Director, InfactCanada/IBFAN North America

Yash Tandon, Director, International South Group Network (Zimbabwe)

Vickey Tauli-Corpuz, Coordinator, Tebtebba (Indigenous Peoples' International Centre for Policy Research and Education)

Etienne Vernet, Food and Agriculture Campaigner Ecoropa (France)

cc: *Mary Robinson*, High Commissioner for Human Rights

Juan Somavia, Director General, International Labour Organisation

Klaus Toepfer, Executive Director, United Nations Environment Programme

Mark Malloch Brown, Administrator, United Nations Development Programme

Carol Bellamy, UNICEF

Georg Kell, First Secretary, Executive Office of the Secretary General

---

July 25, 2000

His Excellency Mr. Kofi Annan
Secretary General
Room 3800
United Nations, NY 10017

Mr. Secretary General,

On July 20th, a number of us wrote asking you to reassess the Global Compact and to join us in a "Citizens Compact." We are writing again today to express our shock upon learning the identities of the corporate partners for the Global Compact and our disappointment in the Guidelines for Cooperation Between the United Nations and the Business Community.

In the July 20th letter, we expressed concern that the U.N. is endorsing a specific vision of corporate-led globalization that is opposed by many sectors of civil society. We also suggested that the purely voluntary nature of the Global Compact may distract from the need for a legal framework to hold corporations accountable internationally.

We wrote to you as individuals who care deeply about the United Nations and on behalf of organizations that have worked for years to strengthen and support it.

Now, after reviewing the July 17th Guidelines and the initial list of companies joining the Global Compact, we believe that the Global Compact and related partnerships threaten the mission and integrity of the United Nations.

Some of the companies in the partnership are simply inappropriate for partnerships with the United Nations.

Nike, one of the Global Compact partners and an international symbol of sweatshops and corporate greed, is the target of one of the most active global campaigns for corporate accountability. The company has made announcements of changes to its behavior only after enormous public pressure. It has also aggressively opposed the only union and human rights–group supported independent monitoring program—the Worker Rights Consortium (WRC). CEO Phil Knight withdrew a $30 million donation to the University of Oregon after the University joined the WRC. Nike also cut its multimillion dollar contracts with the University of Michigan and Brown University after they joined the WRC. Nike became a sweatshop poster child not just through complicity in labor abuses but through active searching for countries with nonunion labor, low wages, and low environmental standards for its manufacturing operations. This has made Nike a leader in the "race to the bottom"—a trend that epitomizes the negative tendencies of corporate-led globalization.

Shell is a corporation with a history of complicity in human rights abuses, most infamously in Nigeria. Its operations there are also notorious for environmental contamination and double standards. Shell has adopted sophisticated rhetoric about its social responsibilities, but it has not shown understanding, let alone remorse, about its own role. For example, on its website, Shell posts a photograph of a pro-Ogoni rally, without acknowledging that the Ogoni people's protests have been against Shell itself.

BP Amoco is another company with sophisticated rhetoric on environmental and social issues. But their actions do not measure up. CEO John Browne admits that climate change is a problem for any oil company, yet his company continues to search for oil and gas even in remote and pristine regions, while investments in renewable energy are a pittance compared with the size of the corporation and its investments in ongoing fossil fuel exploration and production.

Rio Tinto Plc is a British mining corporation which has created so many environment, human rights and development problems that a global network of trade unions, indigenous peoples, church groups, communities and activists has emerged to fight its abuses. For instance, the company stands accused of complicity in or direct violations of environmental, labor and human rights in Indonesia, Papua New Guinea, Philippines, Namibia, Madagascar, the United States and Australia, among others.

Novartis is engaged in an aggressive public relations and regulatory battle to force consumers and farmers to accept genetically engineered food, without full testing for potential harms and without full access to information. The behavior of Novartis in the area of genetically engineered foods is diametrically opposed to the precautionary principle, one of the principles of the Global Compact.

These are but a few of the corporate endorsers of the Global Compact whose historical and current core activities run counter to the spirit and the letter of the Compact itself.

The *Guidelines on Cooperation Between the United Nations and the Business Community* which you issued on July 20th raise a further, related set of issues. These guidelines state that "business entities that are complicit in human rights abuses . . . are not eligible for partnership." The inclusion of Shell in the Global Compact violates those guidelines.

The Guidelines also state that a "business entity may be authorized to use the name and emblem" of the United Nations. As the United Nations Development Programme has noted, when a company uses the U.N. logo, "a mutual image transfer inevitably takes place." It is dismaying to contemplate such an image transfer between Nike, Shell or Rio Tinto and the U.N. The U.N. logo and the Nike swoosh do not belong together.

The Guidelines state that the use of the U.N. name may only be used when the "principal purpose is to show support for the purposes and activities of the U.N. . . ." This guideline does not take into account the modern practice of branding, by which a corporation sells it image as much as its manufactured products. Nike, one of the Global Compact partners, is a pioneer of modern branding. It is obvious that the use of the U.N name and logo by corporations will be not only for short-term profit but for the long term business goal of positive brand image. The U.N. must not become complicit in the positive branding of corporations that violate U.N. principles.

Given that there is no provision for monitoring a corporation's record in abiding by U.N. principles, the Guidelines' modalities for partnerships are quite susceptible to abuse. For example, a company with widespread labor or environmental violations may be able to join with the U.N. in a relatively minor cooperative project, and gain all the benefits of association with the U.N. without any responsibilities. The U.N. would have no way to determine whether the company, on balance, is contributing to U.N. goals or preventing their realization.

In short, Mr. Secretary General, the Global Compact partnership and the Guidelines for Cooperation do not "ensure the integrity and independence" of the United Nations. They allow business entities with poor records to "bluewash" their image by wrapping themselves in the flag of the United Nations. They favor corporate-driven globalization rather than the environment, human health, local communities, workers, farmers, women and the poor.

Again, we urge you to reassess the Global Compact and its partners. We urge you to reevaluate your overall approach to U.N.-corporate partnerships. The mission and integrity of the United Nations are at stake.

Sincerely,

Upendra Baxi, Professor of Law, University of Warwick, U.K. and former Vice Chancellor, University of Delhi (India)

Roberto Bissio, Third World Institute (Uruguay)

John Cavanagh, Director, Institute for Policy Studies (U.S.)

Susan George, Director, Transnational Institute (Netherlands)

Joshua Karliner, Executive Director, CorpWatch (U.S.)

David Korten, President, The People-Centered Development Forum (U.S.)

Miloon Kothari, Coordinator, International NGO Committee on Human Rights in Trade and Investment (India)

Smitu Kothari, President, International Group for Grassroots Initiatives (India)

Jerry Mander, Director, International Forum on Globalization (U.S.)

Remi Parmentier, Director, Political Unit, Greenpeace International (Netherlands)

Atila Roque, Programme Coordinator, Brazilian Institute of Economic and Social Analysis (Brazil)

Elisabeth Sterken, National Director, Infact Canada/IBFAN North America

Victoria Tauli-Corpuz, Executive Director, Tebtebba Foundation (Philippines)

Etienne Vernet, Food and Agriculture Campaigner, Ecoropa (France)

Rob Weissman, Co-director, Essential Action (U.S.)

cc: *Mary Robinson*, High Commissioner for Human Rights

Juan Somavia, Director General, International Labour Organisation

Klaus Toepfer, Executive Director, United Nations Environment Programme

Mark Malloch Brown, Administrator, United Nations Development Programme

Carol Bellamy, UNICEF

Georg Kell, First Secretary, Executive Office of the Secretary General

A letter to Kofi Annan recommending redesign of the Global
Compact from the Alliance for a Corporate-Free U.N.

January 29, 2002

His Excellency Kofi Annan
United Nations, NY 10017
Via fax (212) 963-4879

Dear Mr. Secretary General,

As supporters of the United Nations, we write to you once
again regarding the Global Compact and the U.N.'s private
sector partnership initiatives. We know that your motivation
with the Global Compact is to improve corporate behavior,
and we agree with this goal.

Nevertheless, as we have written in our letters of July 20
and July 25, 2000, shortly before the launch of the Global
Compact, we believe the Compact as currently designed has
serious flaws that threaten the integrity and mission of the
United Nations. In particular, we believe that the Compact
allows companies to improve their reputation through
association with the U.N., without committing to concrete
changes in corporate behavior. It allows these corporations,
and the private sector as a whole, to block substantial
measures for sustainability and accountability—even to
oppose agreements under the framework of the United
Nations itself—while offering only token changes when
convenient.

In addition to fundamental design problems, several
contradictions have come out in the first 18 months of the
Compact's operation. First, while the Global Compact
website claims "transparency" as one of the tools of the
Compact, the corporate membership remains largely secret.
Second, despite repeated avowals that the U.N. logo would
not be misused by corporations under the Global Compact,
at least one company, DaimlerChrysler, has appropriated the
Global Compact logo in its own publication. Third, the
Compact claims learning from case studies as a fundamental
tenet, yet at the first Global Compact Learning Forum last
October, not a single case study was deemed worthy of
publication by the Global Compact Office. Finally, we have
documented violations of one or more Global Compact

principles by five companies that have endorsed the Compact, as well as one major business lobby group.

Documentation of the violations by Aventis, Nike, Unilever, Norsk Hydro, Rio Tinto and the International Chamber of Commerce are attached to this letter. We ask that you ascertain the facts around these cases, and that you act on your findings. We call on you to demand that these companies correct their violations or leave the Global Compact.

Mr. Secretary General, we too believe in the value of dialogue and the wisdom of sharing experiences. Towards the end of creating a more constructive context for these processes, we propose the following redesign of the Global Compact.

1. The full name should be changed to the Global Accountability Compact, to communicate to the public that the ultimate goal is not only to bring private sector activities in line with universal values but to make the private sector accountable to the public.

2. The U.N. should clarify that the Compact is not to be construed as an equal partnership between sectors that share all values and goals. Your Office should further clarify that the Compact's purpose is not to advance a business agenda regarding trade and investment rules.

3. Global Compact companies must agree to support the implementation, and entry into force, of multilateral agreements under U.N. auspices. Without such an agreement, companies can make a mockery of the U.N. by claiming to support it while working behind the scenes to weaken agreements such as the Kyoto Protocol, the Convention on Biodiversity and agreements under the framework of the World Summit on Sustainable Development.

4. The Global Compact's nine principles should be further defined so as to be able to determine whether companies are implementing them or not. A forum should be established to which citizens and NGOs can bring evidence of violations of the principles by Compact companies. The companies could bring their own evidence. The U.N. would determine whether a violation

had occurred, and if so, present the company with a timetable for correcting the violation in order to avoid suspension from the Compact.

5. Global Compact Learning Forum examples and case studies should be open to public review and comment, which should be published along with the corporate contribution. Companies should adopt plans to implement "best practices" at all levels of their company, including international subsidiaries, and publish these plans on the Global Compact website.

6. Your office should undertake a review of the last three decades of corporate-related activity, including lessons from the WHO / UNICEF International Code of Marketing of Breastmilk Substitutes, the increasing interactions of the WHO with the private sector, the UNCTC's work until 1993, UNICEF's ongoing interactions with corporations, etc. This review would form the basis for public evaluation of the advantages and disadvantages of various forms of engagement with the private sector. This in turn could assist in efforts to draft a Convention on Corporate Accountability to be considered by Governments at the World Summit on Sustainable Development in Johannesburg.

These changes would, in our view, constitute an important step in a genuine process of bringing corporate behavior in line with universal values. The promotion of corporate accountability within the U.N. system would be an appropriate and positive use of your personal prestige as a Nobel Prize winner and highly respected Secretary General.

We look forward to your response.

Sincerely,

Walden Bello, Focus on the Global South (Thailand)

John Cavanagh, Institute for Policy Studies (U.S.)

Victoria Corpuz, Tebtebba Foundation (Philippines)

Jocelyn Dow, Women's Environment and Development Organization (U.S.)

Margaret Ewen, Health Action International Europe (Europe)

Susan George, Transnational Institute (Netherlands)

Alvaro Gomez, Renace (Chile)

Olivier Hoedeman, Corporate Europe Observatory (Netherlands)

Joshua Karliner, CorpWatch (U.S.)

David C. Korten, People-Centered Development Forum (Canada)

Smitu Kothari, Lokayan (India)

Chee Yoke Ling, Third World Network (Malaysia)

Alison Linnecar, International Baby Food Action Network (Switzerland / International)

James Paul, Global Policy Forum (U.S.)

Anita Pleumaron, Tourism Investigation and Monitoring Team (Thailand)

Etienne Vernet, Ecoropa (France)

cc: *Mary Robinson*, High Comissioner on Human Rights

    Klaus Toepfer, Executive Director, United Nations Environment Programme

    Mark Malloch-Brown, Administrator, United Nations Development Programme

    Juan Samovia, Director General, International Labour Organization

---

The following Open Letter was sent to U.N. Under-Secretary General Nitin Desai before the start of the third preparatory meeting (Prep-com 3) for the Johannesburg Earth Summit.

Mach 25, 2002

To: Nitin Desai
      United Nations Secretary General of the Johannesburg Summit and Under-Secretary General for Economic and Social Affairs

      United Nations Plaza, Room: DC2-2320
      New York, New York 10017, USA

Dear Under-Secretary General Desai,

The undersigned organizations are supporters of a strong United Nations. We believe in a United Nations which holds commercial interests subservient to human rights, labor and environmental principles, which avoids excessive and undue corporate influence, which holds corporations accountable in a legal framework and which maintains the integrity of international social and environmental agreements.

We are concerned, in particular, with the influence of the International Chamber of Commerce (ICC) and Business Action for Sustainable Development (BASD) on the Johannesburg World Summit on Sustainable Development (WSSD) process. In your speech at the World Economic Forum in January, you described the ICC and the WBCSD as having "embraced the issue" of sustainable development. We think this conclusion is premature and gives these groups an undeserved seal of approval.

We would like to call your attention to the risk of assuming that certain corporate lobby groups are truly committed to sustainable development, when in fact they have failed to "walk the talk." We believe that such assumptions give the incorrect impression that entrenched, unsustainable patterns of production and consumption led by global business are well on the way to resolution. These assumptions send out the message that big business has proven itself as an ally and partner and that there is no need for further action by the world's governments to prevent corporations from damaging the environment and sustainable development.

Particularly in the case of the ICC, there is a disturbing gap between their self-proclaimed commitment and the reality of a consistent record of lobbying to block, postpone or weaken progress in international negotiations on issues of crucial importance to sustainable development. Examples include the Basel Convention on trade in toxic waste, the Kyoto Protocol and the Convention on Biodiversity. We enclose a July 2001 report ("High Time for UN to Break 'Partnership' with the ICC"), which documents how the ICC with its obstructive lobbying has violated key principles of the Global Compact, which the ICC joined from the start.

While it is obviously important to encourage business to abandon unsustainable practices, it is counterproductive to congratulate corporate lobby groups on their commitment before they have taken the minimum necessary steps towards contributing to sustainable development. One such step is obviously to break with irresponsible lobbying practices, which hinder the development of effective international treaties to bring business practices in line with sustainable development. The U.N. has a key role to play in making it clear to international business that obstructing progress in international negotiations must be put to an end.

The credibility of the ICC`s claimed commitment to sustainable development is furthermore seriously undermined by its opposition to binding corporate accountability mechanisms. The ICC continues to promote an unbalanced and unsustainable economic model of global market deregulation in which corporate rights are carved in stone while corporate responsibilities remain voluntary. This approach has proven entirely insufficient in the decade since the Rio summit. The ICC, in its role as an early-stage codesigner of the Global Compact, has also seriously weakened that initiative by insisting on keeping it free of monitoring and enforcement. We remind you that the ICC arrogantly abandoned the Voluntary Initiatives Project of the Commission for Sustainable Development (CSD) in order to escape the inconvenient conclusions that were likely to have come out of this assessment.

The proposal to start negotiations on a U.N. corporate accountability convention has surfaced as a key demand from civil society for the Johannesburg Summit. If the ICC and its member corporations had a genuine, long-term commitment to sustainable development, surely they would not oppose measures to make responsible conduct obligatory for all international business. We believe that such support is a litmus test for corporate lobby groups like the ICC, the WBCSD and their new offspring Business Action for Sustainable Development (BASD). As long as these groups continue to campaign against effective international mechanisms to ensure corporate accountability, they cannot be said to have embraced sustainable development in anything but words.

We hope you will use every opportunity to raise this key issue in the preparations for the Johannesburg Summit. Only if real progress is made in addressing the current corporate accountability vacuum can Rio+10 become the success we all hope for.

Yours sincerely,

Philipp Mimkes, Coalition Against BAYER Dangers, Germany

Kenny Bruno, CorpWatch, U.S.

Olivier Hoedeman, Corporate Europe Observatory (CEO), Netherlands

Ward Morehouse, Council on International and Public Affairs, U.S.

Katie Redford, Co-director, EarthRights International, Thailand/U.S.

Annabell Waititu, Environment Liaison Centre International (ELCI), Kenya

Matt Phillips, Friends of the Earth England, Wales and Northern Ireland

Bobby Peek, groundWork, South Africa

Allison Linnecar, IBFAN/GIFA, Switzerland

John Cavanagh, Institute for Policy Studies, U.S.

Roberto Bissio, Instituto del Tercer Mundo, Uruguay

Yash Tandon, International South Group Network (ISGN)

Jane Dennett-Thorpe, Inzet, Netherlands

Paul de Clerck, Milieudefensie (Friends of the Earth), Netherlands

Syed Naeem Bukhari, Executive Director, NOOR, Pakistan

David C. Korten, People-Centered Development Forum, U.S.

Michael Dorsey, Director, Sierra Club National Board, U.S.

Chee Yoke Ling, Third World Network, Malaysia

Susan George and Fiona Dove, Transnational Institute, Netherlands

Emmy Hafield, Executive Director, WAHLI (Friends of the Earth), Indonesia

Alliance for Democracy, U.S.

A SEED, Europe

Christian Aid, U.K.

The CornerHouse, U.K.

DAWN (Development Alternatives with Women for a New Era), Fiji

Friends of the Earth, Sweden

Grassroots Globalization Network, U.S.

The Greens/EFA Group in the European Parliament (45 Members of the European Parliament, from 12 E.U. member countries)

Index

Globalization
   environmental and development
      problems and, 5, 11–12
   give a human face to, 49
   since Rio Earth Summit, 6–8
   technology transfer and, 12–13, 35
   worldwide movement challenging,
      20–21, 50–51, 60, 61–62, 73
Global Sustainable Development
   Facility (GSDF), 45–48
Global warming, 5, 10, 12, 16, 17,
   37–39, 108–9. *See also* Carbon
   dioxide emissions
Goldman Sachs, 43
Goluke, Ulrich, 31
Greenpeace, x, 4, 6, 84, 109
Greenwash
   classic, 77
   common forms of, 81–82
   deep, 78
   definition of, 78
   snapshots of, 82–109
*Guidelines on Cooperation Between the
   United Nations and the Business
   Community,* 55, 153–54
Gunther, Herbert Chao, 89

H

Habitat for Humanity, 59
Halliburton, 9
Hansen, Peter, 26
Heroes for the Planet Concert, 92
Hill and Knowlton, 24, 92
Human rights violations, 16, 18, 48,
   110–16
Human Rights Watch, 53
Hunger, 97–98

I

Imle, John, 48
India, 34, 112–13
Indonesia, 111
Indonesian People's Forum, 4
Infact, 103
Institute for Policy Studies, 30
International Baby Food Action
   Network, 19, 23
International Center for Alcohol
   Policies (ICAP), 54

International Chamber of Commerce
   (ICC), 7, 9, 14, 17, 28, 29, 30,
   31, 38, 43, 52–53, 63, 112, 157,
   160–61
International Code of Marketing of
   Breastmilk Substitutes, 23–24
International Monetary Fund (IMF),
   9, 21

J

Japan, 8, 25, 36
Johannesburg Earth Summit, x, 4,
   17–18, 20, 57–59, 62–63, 73,
   115, 159, 161

K

Kelian mine, 111–12
Kell, Georg, 54
Kernaghan, Charles, 49
Khor, Martin, 11, 12, 29, 51–52, 61
King, Martin Luther, Jr., 68
Knight, Phil, 40, 152
Kodaikanal, India, 112–13
Kraft, 102–3
Kyoto Protocol, 12, 16–18, 37–39, 73,
   107, 108, 112, 160

L

Laguna San Ignacio, 93–97
Lindahl, Goran, 65

M

Malloch-Brown, Mark, 47
Marrakech, 8
McDonalds, 43
Mexico, 9–10, 93, 96, 111
Mining industry, 111–12, 113, 153
Mitsubishi, 93–97
Monsanto, 37, 86, 97–99
Montreal Protocol, 12, 32–33
Moody Stuart, Mark, 17–18, 58
Moyers, Bill, 42
Multilateral Agreement on
   Investment, 69
Multinational Monitor, 114–15

Acknowledgments

A lot of people helped make this book possible and we will inevitably forget to thank some of them. But here's our best shot. Thanks to our friends at International Baby Food Action Network, Institute for Policy Studies, Coalition Against Bayer Dangers, Third World Network, Greenpeace International, Friends of the Earth International, Global Exchange, Project Underground, groundWork and Corporate Europe Observatory, and to all the members of the Alliance for a Corporate-Free U.N. for all the analysis, information, political vision and organizing around these issues. Thanks to our friends inside the United Nations. Thanks to the entire staff and board of CorpWatch—especially to Nadia Khastagir—for all the effort around this project and the years of work that led up to it. Thanks to Jim Vallette, Richard Sherman, Ward Morehouse and Li Lin. Thanks to the CarEth and JMG Foundations for their specific support for our work on the U.N. and thanks to all the other CorpWatch supporters who helped make this book a reality through their generosity. Thanks to everyone at Food First, especially our editor Clancy Drake and co-directors Anuradha Mittal and Peter Rosset for believing in the project. And thanks to our families for putting up with our foolhardy notion that we could do this thing so quickly!

—KB and JK

About the Authors

Kenny Bruno currently works with CorpWatch on its U.N. project and with Earth Rights International on human rights environmental issues, and teaches strategic campaigning and advocacy at New York University. Kenny worked with Greenpeace for more than twelve years on a variety of domestic and international toxics issues. He has also worked on sweatshop issues for the National Labor Committee and served on the international steering committee of Oil Watch, an Ecuador-based network of resistance to oil development in the tropics. He is co-author of *Greenwash: The Reality Behind Corporate Environmentalism* (Third World Network/Apex Press, 1996), and his writing has also appeared in the *International Herald Tribune*, the *San Francisco Chronicle* and the *Oregonian*.

Joshua Karliner is founder and executive director of CorpWatch. He has taught global environmental politics at the University of San Francisco and served as Earth Summit coordinator for Greenpeace International in 1992. He co-founded and served as director of the Environmental Project on Central America (EPOCA), then a project of Earth Island Institute. He is author of *The Corporate Planet: Ecology and Politics in the Age of Globalization* (Sierra Club Books, 1997). His writing has appeared in the *Washington Post*, the *International Herald Tribune*, the *San Francisco Chronicle*, the *Journal of Commerce*, *The Nation*, *World Policy Journal* and a wide array of environmental magazines.

CORPWATCH
Holding Corporations Accountable
www.corpwatch.org

www.CorpWatch.org

CorpWatch.org is *the* Internet gateway for progressive information on human rights and the environmental impacts of transnational corporations. CorpWatch.org provides the tools people need to research corporations, to obtain progressive news and analysis on globalization issues, and to take action.

Climate Justice Initiative

We are helping to build a movement for climate justice— one that aims to hold corporations accountable by bringing local grassroots initiatives for human rights and environmental justice together with international efforts to protect the world's climate.

CorpWatch India

CorpWatch India helps foster action internationally and strengthen the movements countering corporate globalization in India. Its innovative website, CorpWatchIndia.org, provides news, analysis, and research tools.

CorpWatch counters corporate-led globalization through education and activism. We work to foster democratic control over corporations by building grassroots globalization —a diverse movement for human rights, labor rights, and environmental justice.

Alliance for a Corporate-Free U.N.

CorpWatch is the secretariat for a global alliance of organizations and networks that expose the U.N.'s increasing entanglement with corporations. We are pressuring the U.N. to fulfill its mission for human, labor, and environmental rights by working to hold corporations accountable to these values.

Greenwash Awards

CorpWatch presents Greenwash Awards to corporations that put more money, time, and energy into slick PR campaigns aimed at promoting their eco-friendly images than into actually protecting the environment. Nominations for these awards come from our audience.

www.earthsummit.biz

This spoof website reveals the greenwashing of the Johannesburg Earth Summit 2002. Readers can vote online to nominate the top offending corporations for the Greenwash Academy Awards.

CorpWatch • PO Box 29344 • San Francisco, CA 94129 • USA
t: +1 415-561-6568 • f: +1 415-561-6493 • e: cwadmin@corpwatch.org

ABOUT FOOD FIRST

Food First, also known as the Institute for Food and Development Policy, is a nonprofit research and education-for-action center dedicated to investigating and exposing the root causes of hunger in a world of plenty. It was founded in 1975 by Frances Moore Lappé, author of the bestseller *Diet for a Small Planet,* and food policy analyst Dr. Joseph Collins. Food First research has revealed that hunger is created by concentrated economic and political power, not by scarcity. Resources and decision-making are in the hands of a wealthy few, depriving the majority of land, jobs, and therefore food.

Hailed by the *New York Times* as "one of the most established food think tanks in the country," Food First has grown to profoundly shape the debate about hunger and development.

But Food First is more than a think tank. Through books, reports, videos, media appearances, and speaking engagements, Food First experts not only reveal the often hidden roots of hunger, they show how individuals can get involved in bringing an end to the problem. Food First inspires action by bringing to light the courageous efforts of people around the world who are creating farming and food systems that truly meet people's needs.

HOW TO BECOME A MEMBER OR INTERN OF FOOD FIRST

BECOME A MEMBER OF FOOD FIRST

Private contributions and membership gifts form the financial base of Food First/Institute for Food and Development Policy. The success of the Institute's programs depends not only on its dedicated volunteers and staff, but on financial activists as well. Each member strengthens Food First's efforts to change a hungry world. We invite you to join Food First. As a member you will receive a twenty percent discount on all Food First books. You will also receive our quarterly publication, *Food First News and Views,* and timely *Backgrounders* that provide information and suggestions for action on current food and hunger crises in the United States and around the world. If you want to subscribe to our Internet newsletters, *Food Rights Watch* and *We Are Fighting Back,* send us an email at foodfirst@foodfirst.org. All contributions are tax-deductible.

BECOME AN INTERN FOR FOOD FIRST

There are opportunities for interns in research, advocacy, campaigning, publishing, computers, media, and publicity at Food First. Our interns come from around the world. They are a vital part of our organization and make our work possible.

To become a member or apply to become an intern, just call, visit our web site, or clip and return the attached coupon to

Food First/Institute for Food and Development Policy
398 60th Street, Oakland, CA 94618, USA
PHONE: 510.654.4400 FAX: 510.654.4551
EMAIL: foodfirst@foodfirst.org
WEB SITE: www.foodfirst.org

You are also invited to give a gift membership to others interested in the fight to end hunger.

JOINING FOOD FIRST

☐ I want to join Food First and receive a 20% discount on this and all subsequent orders. Enclosed is my tax-deductible contribution of:

☐ $35   ☐ $50   ☐ $100   ☐ $1,000   ☐ OTHER

NAME _____

ADDRESS _____

CITY/STATE/ZIP _____

DAYTIME PHONE (_____) _____

E-MAIL _____

ORDERING FOOD FIRST MATERIALS

ITEM DESCRIPTION	QTY	UNIT COST	TOTAL

PAYMENT METHOD:

☐ CHECK

☐ MONEY ORDER

☐ MASTERCARD

☐ VISA

MEMBER DISCOUNT, 20% $ _____

CA RESIDENTS SALES TAX 8.25% $ _____

SUBTOTAL $ _____

POSTAGE 15%   UPS: 20%   ($2 MIN.) $ _____

MEMBERSHIP(S) $ _____

ADDITIONAL CONTRIBUTION $ _____

TOTAL ENCLOSED $ _____

_____
NAME ON CARD

_____
CARD NUMBER   EXP. DATE

_____
SIGNATURE

MAKE CHECK OR MONEY ORDER PAYABLE TO:

FOOD FIRST, 398 – 60TH STREET, OAKLAND, CA 94618

FOOD FIRST GIFT BOOKS

Please send a Gift Book to (order form on reverse side):

NAME _____

ADDRESS _____

CITY/STATE/ZIP _____

FROM _____

FOOD FIRST PUBLICATIONS CATALOGS

Please send a Publications Catalog to:

NAME _____

ADDRESS _____

CITY/STATE/ZIP _____

NAME _____

ADDRESS _____

CITY/STATE/ZIP _____

NAME _____

ADDRESS _____

CITY/STATE/ZIP _____

FOOD FIRST GIFT MEMBERSHIPS

☐ Enclosed is my tax-deductible contribution of:

☐ $35   ☐ $50   ☐ $100   ☐ $1,000   ☐ OTHER

Please send a Food First membership to:

NAME _____

ADDRESS _____

CITY/STATE/ZIP _____

FROM _____

MORE BOOKS FROM FOOD FIRST

Sustainable Agriculture and Development: Transforming Food Production in Cuba
Fernando Funes, Luis García, Martin Bourque, Nilda Pérez, and Peter Rosset
Unable to import food or farm chemicals and machines in the wake of the Soviet bloc's collapse and a tightening U.S. embargo, Cuba turned toward sustainable agriculture, organic farming, urban gardens, and other techniques to secure its food supply. This book gives details of that remarkable achievement.
Paperback, $18.95

The Future in the Balance: Essays on Globalization and Resistance
Walden Bello
Edited with a preface by Anuradha Mittal
A new collection of essays by Third World activist and scholar Walden Bello on the myths of development as prescribed by the World Trade Organization and other institutions, and the possibility of another world based on fairness and justice.
Paperback, $13.95

Views from the South: The Effects of Globalization and the WTO on Third World Countries
Foreword by Jerry Mander
Afterword by Anuradha Mittal
Edited by Sarah Anderson
This rare collection of essays by Third World activists and scholars describes in pointed detail the effects of the WTO and other Bretton Woods institutions.
Paperback, $12.95

Basta! Land and the Zapatista Rebellion in Chiapas
Revised edition
George A. Collier with Elizabeth Lowery Quaratiello
Foreword by Peter Rosset
The classic on the Zapatistas in a new revised edition, including a preface by Roldolfo Stavenhagen, a new epilogue about the present challenges to the indigenous movement in Chiapas, and an updated bibliography.
Paperback, $14.95

America Needs Human Rights
Edited by Anuradha Mittal and Peter Rosset
This new anthology includes writings on understanding human rights, poverty in America, and welfare reform and human rights.
Paperback, $13.95

The Paradox of Plenty: Hunger in a Bountiful World
Excerpts from Food First's best writings on world hunger and what we can do to change it.
Paperback, $18.95

A Siamese Tragedy: Development and Disintegration in Modern Thailand
Walden Bello, Shea Cunningham, and Li Kheng Poh
Critiques the failing economic system that has propelled the Thai people down an unstable path.
Paperback, $19.95

Dark Victory: The United States and Global Poverty
Walden Bello, with Shea Cunningham and Bill Rau
Second edition, with a new epilogue by the author
Offers an understanding of why poverty has deepened in many countries, and analyzes the impact of U.S. economic policies.
Paperback, $14.95

Education for Action: Graduate Studies with a Focus on Social Change
Fourth edition
Edited by Joan Powell
A newly updated authoritative and easy-to-use guidebook that provides information on progressive programs in a wide variety of fields.
Paperback, $12.95

Alternatives to the Peace Corps: A Directory of Third World and U.S. Volunteer Opportunities
Ninth edition
Edited by Joan Powell
Over one hundred listings of organizations in the United States and the Third World provide prospective volunteers an array of choices to make their commitment count.
Paperback, $9.95

Food First books are available through most bookstores and national and regional wholesalers. Individuals may order books online at our website, www.foodfirst.org. If you have trouble locating a Food First title, write, call, or email us:

Food First
398 60th Street
Oakland, CA 94618, USA
PHONE: 510.654.4400 FAX: 510.654.4551
EMAIL: foodfirst@foodfirst.org
WEB SITE: www.foodfirst.org